# FINDING
# MY
# VOICE

# FINDING
# MY
# VOICE

*a memoir*

# REBECCA THOMAS

TATE PUBLISHING & *Enterprises*

Published by Tate Publishing & Enterprises, LLC
127 E. Trade Center Terrace | Mustang, Oklahoma 73064 USA
1.888.361.9473 | www.tatepublishing.com

Tate Publishing is committed to excellence in the publishing industry. The company reflects the philosophy established by the founders, based on Psalm 68:11,
*"The Lord gave the word and great was the company of those who published it."*

Published in the United States of America

ISBN: 978-1-61346-091-7
Biography & Autobiography / Personal Memoirs
11.08.17

This book is dedicated to those who have yet to discover their own voice. Realize that what you are going through now is only a small part of your life and that with a little hope and faith, you'll make it through.

# ACKNOWLEDGEMENTS

To my parents, Albina and Francis, you will never know how much I love you. If I had all the money in the world, I still would not be able to repay you for all you have sacrificed for me. Thank you does not begin to cover it, but it is what I have, so thank you.

To Hannah, even though we still fight sometimes, you are the best answer to prayer I could have gotten. I love you.

To Glenn, Junior, and Tony—while two of you can be annoying at times (you know which ones you are), I know you guys do it out of love and will always be there for me. Love you guys.

To Akisha, Neela, Juliette, Ayana, Jeremy, Marisa, Micah, Angie, Junny, Gerard, Pearl, and Jaleel—you are my extended family and nieces and nephews; I love you all.

To those who may not have received a name mention or maybe just a short appearance, your presence and influence in my life is appreciated. You all have played a part in who I have become as a woman. I thank you from the bottom of my heart.

To everyone at Tate publishing—you have all made this an enjoyable process. I appreciate the effort that each of you put into my book, even from the very beginning. You believed in my book and it made me believe in it. Thank you for everything.

# PROLOGUE

Many of us know what it's like to be on the outside looking in, to be judged because of how you look, to be told that you couldn't do it or wouldn't make it, and the list goes on. This book isn't about what you should or shouldn't do. The real lesson can be found in learning that no matter what identity you find, you should be proud of it, no matter what anyone else thinks.

Everyone has a story, but not all are heard. Many find themselves being quieted by those who did not want to make waves or cause discomfort for others. For too long I have been made to be quiet, but no more. I learned long ago that there were times when my mouth would fail me and words would cease. I would discover that the pen could be my voice and sometimes it was the best way to express how I felt. Here is my story as it happened, so far.

# CHAPTER ONE

*Ten years from now, most of what we freak out about won't make any difference.*

—*Anonymous*

My story begins in 1984, where I was born on the island of St. Croix to St. Lucian parents and into a family with three older siblings. Bradley was the oldest and would leave for the navy by the time I was three. Next there was Jack. He was definitely the quietest of my three brothers. I always felt a special bond to him because our temperaments were fairly similar. Lastly, there was CJ, by far the craziest. And since he was closest to me in age, we spent much of my childhood together; that meant we fought a lot.

I would only live on that wonderful island for the first five years of my life because my dad would be called to be a pastor and transplant his family to Jacksonville, Florida. My parents had only been Christians for a short time before my birth, and by the time a year in Florida had passed, we moved to West Columbia, South Carolina. It was also in that year that my mom would give birth to my sister, Leah. I was excited because I prayed so hard for a sister. There would be times in the years to come that I would wonder what I was thinking (in the most loving way). We moved because Dad was contacted by a church there to come up and start a black church in the area. I can't help but look back now and wonder why it had to be race specific, but we will get to that later.

It is here that the story really begins, and to spare you the boredom that is the early years, we are going to skip forward to 1997. Looking back, it seems so long ago…

T he church that sent for my dad while we were in Jacksonville was now our home church. Dad's church was going well for a while, but eventually the number of people that were coming became smaller and smaller. It soon came to the point where there just were not enough people to support the church. I had been going to their private school ever since we arrived in the area. Mom had worked in their daycare from that time and Leah had been attending since she was a baby.

This was the year it was all supposed to change. I was a freshman! Now for most schools that meant small fish in a big pond, but not mine. Junior high and high school were combined into one, so really, the seventh graders were the small fish. Now we had some power. As ninth graders, we could push around the junior high kids and feel some sense of worth. At least that is how it felt.

I had spent the past seven years with the same friends. Chloe, Lorie, Rachel, Gail, Dana, and I had been good friends since elementary. We were known as the goody-two shoes or teachers' pets by the rest of our classmates. Chloe, who was my best friend, was the beauty of the group. She looked like an Indian princess, and need-less to say, all the guys loved her. I had spent my time as her friend being the liaison between her and guys who wanted to date her. For some strange reason, I actually enjoyed this role.

Next there was Lorie. If we were the goody-two shoes, she was the queen of us all. Teachers saw her as the prime example of what a well-behaved student should have been like. Rachel was a quiet force. She was one of the few in our class along with Chloe and Lorie that was a cheerleader. She also attracted the guys with her dark hair and glasses. While Chloe was my best friend, I always felt I had the best bond with Rachel. Dana was the blonde of the group and threw a wrench in the teacher's pet concept of our group. She had a wild streak that she managed to keep under control while we were in school. Lastly, there was Gail. With her reddish brown hair, she was the quietest of us all. She was probably the smartest of us all, but like me, she found it difficult to find her place in high school.

Did I mention that this was a predominately white school and church? This didn't mean a thing to me because my parents had taught me to love everyone, but as an island girl coming into the South, I had no idea about the racial tension that my family had entered. There were only four other black people in the high school, and we were pretty much the minorities in the school. My good friend Tabitha made up the other faction of the minority as she was half-Asian and half-Caucasian.

With this new school year, that meant new students and that meant new kids in my class, two to be exact, and one just happened to be a black boy. Students and faculty alike were acting as if I had hit the jack pot. Why was it they automatically tried to set him up with me? He could be perfect for anyone else in my class, or even the whole school, but since they only saw color, we obviously were meant to be. To protest only meant that I really liked him deep down inside. It was difficult dealing with the prejudice considering that at that time I developed a crush on this other guy in my class, Ryan. I had easily learned that my "type" of guy was the tall, great tan, and handsome type. Ryan fit all three. His dark hair and olive skin tone definitely made this girl drool. Okay, so not literally, but point proven. Either way, I just wanted everyone to get a good dose of reality and realize that liking someone had nothing to do with skin color and everything to do with who they were on the inside. My philosophy: Look for Prince Charming on the inside, and you will find that there is a Prince Charming on the outside.

I decided that after two years of pretty much coasting by, I was going to get out there and be involved in my school. I mean, it was the best school in the world! Up until then, the only thing I was involved in was the school band. Well, we all know that most people see that as the activity for geeks. In my school if it was the only thing you were involved in, then yes, you were a geek. But with our student body size, it was not a surprise to find the star of the soccer team playing the trumpet in the band.

There was only one problem—okay, maybe two. First, I was painfully shy. At the end of the sixth grade, we were able to try out for the cheerleading squad. This was a *big* deal. It would be the start of anyone's social existence. Every girl (with the exception of the tomboy in the class) tried out for the squad. Okay, so there were only about twelve or so girls in the class, but you get how important it was, right? Only five made the junior high squad, and that brought me to my second problem. I was a little overweight. By that, I mean most of the girls were size zero or two and I was a six or eight. To compound on this, I was the youngest in the class. If you went by age, I should have technically been in the class below us, but I was able to start school early back when we were in St. Croix. Anyway, one could already see the problem. By my freshman year, I was a size twelve to fourteen and feeling deeply insecure. I figured I would try out for the squad again because evidently I loved pain and embarrassment. After the first day, I quickly realized that I was going to have to find another way to make my mark. When Chloe, Lorie, and Rachel became cheerleaders, Gail, Dana, and I were left to fend for ourselves. The three of us did pick up playing instruments, but like I said, that wasn't much help in achieving my ultimate goal of social prominence. Lorie played in the band as well, but she was a cheerleader, so it did not matter.

With the size of my school, extracurricular activities were limited. I needed some sport to add to my band geek stature to elevate to athlete/musician. Sports in my school were what could make or break you socially. That left me with only two choices: volleyball or basketball. Technically, it left me with only one choice, as it was just the beginning of the year and that meant it was volleyball season. Basketball did not start until after volleyball season was over. My plan seemed well thought out, but tryouts for the team occurred while my family and I were on vacation. Rachel talked with the coach while I was on vacation and let her know just how much I wanted to try out. Thankfully, the coach was kind enough to make me the scorekeeper/manager of the team. More plainly, I was the gopher. Thankfully, the girls on the team treated me pretty well, so it wasn't all that bad.

The good thing about being team manager was I got to go on all the away games. I know what some are thinking—how exciting can that really be? If there was one thing I learned by not being socially active, it was that all the good stories and events happened on the bus going and coming back from places. I wanted the inside scoop, and I finally had the chance to get it. Not only was Tabby on the team, but Chloe, Lorie, and Rachel were getting to experience the social benefits for two years now as cheerleaders—it was my turn. I spent that season absorbing as much as I could around me. It was amazing what people would say when they thought I wasn't listening. I quickly learned who liked who, who wanted to date or breakup, and many of the other tidbits around me. I never thought of myself as naïve, but those bus trips were eye-openers.

Eventually, it seemed that all in my class had figured out my crush on Ryan. That led to merciless teasing at any chance they had. This also produced some girl's catty side. She would make comments to purposely make me jealous. If I did something to stand out, the next day she was doing the same thing. I was trying my hardest to stay true to who I was and just to be myself. It was frustrating that some were being who they were not. I didn't want to end up like that; I knew the only thing it would lead to was disappointment. I didn't want to be like so many and throw myself at a guy just to get him to notice me. Conveniently enough, my family had moved only a few houses down from where he and his family lived. I saw this as a sign from God. We were meant to be! I looked at every gesture, smile, time we talked—whatever I could for some clue as to how he may have felt about me.

Soon homecoming was approaching, and it was everyone's favorite time of year—picking the homecoming representative for the class. This was supposed to be an individual selection process, but ever since my class got into junior high, one of the popular guys in our class would pick one girl and tell everyone that was who we were voting for. That year, they decided it was going to be me. I couldn't have been more thrilled, except I was a size twelve living in a size-two world. While I had lost some weight over the summer, I still was not "perfect." I figured if I could find the perfect dress, maybe Ryan would notice me and my chances might just go up.

Living in a size-two world had its disadvantages. My mom and I went from store to store, looking for dresses for me, but we were quickly finding that every store seemed to have more of the same dresses that were in the previous stores. All those dresses had one thing in common—they were not made for girls with curves. Talk about your disappointment. As I was about to give up, my mom (my hero) found a nice, albeit not what I was looking for, white and black dress. I still figured that night would be great. I mean, only eight girls in our junior high and high school years would get to be on the court, and they picked me. I should have been thankful!

I arrived that night, and the princess treatment began. I had my photo taken by myself and then one with my dad. They handed us our flowers, and we waited for halftime of the varsity guy's game. The lights dimmed in the gym, and we lined up for our processional into the gym. I was nervous. Dad would say to me later how he could feel my arm shaking in his. The seventh- and eighth-grade representatives went out, and I waited by the door with my dad for them to call my name. When they did, I walked with my dad on my arm, soaking in every moment. I couldn't see out into the crowd as it was dark and a spotlight was on us. The only thing I could tell was that people were cheering and clapping. It was my moment to feel special and truly cared about. I knew that even in the years to come, if I did not complete my social supremacy, I would always have this moment. My moment in the spotlight was soon over, and thankfully it turned out to be a wonderful night, no matter how much I disliked my dress (not to mention one of the other girls was wearing the dress I could not get my hips into). I truly felt like a princess.

All of the dress drama from homecoming inspired me to do something about my weight. It was another part of my plan to fit in socially. I was convinced Ryan didn't like me because I was fat. Unfortunately, my friend Gail and I had a falling out, and in her attempt to get back at me, she asked Ryan what my chances were. Sadly, I would learn they were less than 5 percent—talk about heartbreak. With the current standing, over the semester, my feelings for Ryan dissipated, and I thankfully could call him a friend. I came to realize how stupid I was when it came to him and how I acted sometimes. He would go on to become one of my great guy friends.

As a part of my social networking and eager attempt to overcome my painful shyness, I decided to give acting a try. It was now March, and tryouts for the annual school play were occurring. Why not? I had nothing to lose. Much to my surprise, the drama coach thought I was good, and I got a callback. It was now a senior and I who were up for the part of an old lady. While I was good, seniority ruled when it came to everything, and the senior got the part. I was not upset because I didn't think I could have really done it. I mean, I would have to talk in front of a room full of people. The thought scared me. All I wanted was to be a part of the experience in some way. I ended up being behind the scenes doing the makeup, which kept me close enough to the socially advanced. My plan was going smoothly.

t was now May, and I had gone from a size fourteen to a size nine. I felt great. Awards Day was just around the corner, and I felt it was necessary to have a new dress for such a special day. I wasn't completely sure why I felt this way, as the only awards I normally received were Honor Roll and occasionally the highest average in one of the subjects. I was so happy to go into the dressing room of a store and find that a size nine fit me like a glove. Unfortunately, the beautiful dress that I had on and had fallen in love with I could not have. Mom and Dad said there was just no money for it. I was bummed to say the least, but I understood. Money didn't exactly fly around for two people involved in the church ministry. Awards Day arrived, and much to my surprise, Mom and Dad had a present for me. I opened the box, and I was delighted to lift out the very dress I had fallen in love with a few days before. I *knew* that day would be great. I was right too. I received certificates for top grades in two of my classes and the best award: outstanding student of the year. Normally that award went to Gail or Lorie. It was the one and only time I received that award. It was my year!

With the end of school, it meant summer was finally here. I felt I had accomplished a lot in my quest for social supremacy. I mean, I was a part of the volleyball team, made the homecoming court, and was involved in the school play. On top of all of that, I had lost some weight. For a fourteen-year-old, that was a pretty big deal. I decided to continue my weight loss throughout the summer and get in shape for the upcoming volleyball season.

Dana had been coming over to help me train during the day. Our training was also going to help me when it came time to start PE and I had to run the mile. I had never been able to run the mile in the necessary time, but for my last year of PE—my sophomore year—I was determined to succeed.

Ryan had a younger sister named Angelina—Angie for short. Angie had the same olive complexion as her brother and the same dark hair. If her older sister was any indication, she would be a stunner soon enough. She was two years younger than me, and since she would be a junior high student in the fall, I figured I could help to make the transition a smooth one. (I knew I wished someone had done the same for me.) Now this would seem to be easy enough as we lived in the same neighborhood, but Angie was a little weary of me. I didn't blame her; we got off on the wrong foot only a few months ago. I had to make up for it. I invited her over to practice volleyball in hopes that maybe she too would try out and make it. All in all that year went pretty well, and I couldn't wait to see what next year had for me.

# CHAPTER TWO

*When you have nothing left but God, then for the first time you become aware that God is enough.*
—*Maude Royden*

It was a new school year and a new me. I was happy to say I was walking into school that year as a size four. I would finally fit into the world around me. It had become an obsession with me. Every time I looked into a mirror, I saw something that needed to be changed. There was always an area that needed to be improved because there was just too much fat. The compliments I was receiving helped to ease the pain because I felt as if I was finally being accepted and getting the approval of those I thought were important. With the compliments came the question of how I lost the weight. There was no real secret—change in diet and regular exercise and probably the fact that I was shedding 'baby fat.' It was all a part of growing up, I assumed. I had even had one guy tell me I looked good enough to date, but he couldn't because I was black and he was white. Stifling back the anger, I accepted the semi-compliment. I would take what I could get, I guess.

The dynamics in my group of friends had changed drastically over the summer. Rachel had moved to North Carolina; Chloe had gone "popular" on us; Lorie had changed so much I didn't know how to describe her; things with Gail were tense at best, and Dana and I had grown closer than ever. In fact, with all the time that Dana spent at my house over the summer, Dana, Ryan, and I had become almost inseparable. With all that went on the previous year, it didn't surprise me much when people mistook my bond with Ryan for me having feelings for him. The only thing was that I was getting tired of being asked that question over and over again. He had become something like my best friend. Then again, is it not said that building a friendship is the best way to start a relationship? I had to keep reminding myself that I was only a sophomore in high school and that I had to be patient. Whenever it was time for me to have a boyfriend, that was when I would get one. It just didn't help much that everyone else around me was in and out of relationships like they changed their socks.

Volleyball season had started, and this time, I was actually on the team! My social status was only increasing. I had also decided to join the yearbook staff. The people on the yearbook staff had inside information, so that meant it would only help me achieve my ultimate goal. This was also my last year of PE, and with that came the dreaded mile. For three years it beat me, but I had trained and I was ready. I hoped. The day came for recording the official times, and Dana said she would run along with me. For the most part we stayed together. I got to the final lap, and Dana finished a good forty seconds or so before me. I came to the final turn, and Dana came back to me and encouraged me to finish. This was what we worked for all summer long. I crossed the finish line, and I waited for the moment of truth. For my age, I had to finish the mile just under eight minutes. The question was: had I? Our PE coach (who was also the volleyball head coach) read my final time—7:44. I had done it! Dana and I were jumping up and down in excitement. I accomplished what I had set out to do, and I knew I could not have done it without Dana's help.

Volleyball season was coming to an end, but not before one of the most anticipated social outings of the year— the state fair. By now, Gail and I had patched things up, so it was nice to have her with us as well as Ryan and a few other friends. While one could attend the fair with their family, it was a completely different experience when you got to go with your friends. I was too excited for words and nervous beyond belief. I was too much of a chicken to go on any of the rides, but everyone else would be going on them. What was I to do? For some odd reason, I found the courage to go on almost every ride that they went on. Or could it have been that I had made a promise to Ryan that I would ride some rides? The night couldn't have been any better than at sunset, when we found ourselves on the giant Ferris wheel. (Did I mention that I'm afraid of heights?)

We stopped at the top, and the view was amazing, with the sun sitting just at the horizon. Being surrounded by most of my good friends, I couldn't have pictured a better way to end the evening, well almost. The group 98 Degrees was in concert at the grandstand. Unfortunately, our school forbade us from going to concerts—the penalty being severe punishment or expulsion. My friends and I, being the sad, boy-band-loving group that we were, found an empty wall and took turns putting each other on our shoulders so we could just get a glimpse of the guys in concert. That only lasted a few minutes until the security guards came to tell us to move away from the wall. What a night!

In accordance with my plan of social supremacy, I decided that for our annual private school state competition, I was going to do a speech duet with Dana. I dare say that our time spent together during the summer had drawn us closer as friends. She had just started dating a friend of mine, Philip, and she just wanted to spend some time with him. We decided to plan a double date of sorts. She came over and spent the night at my house, and Philip spent the night at Ryan's. The guys came over, and we enjoyed popcorn, pizza, and a movie. The night was going smoothly; that is until it came time to watch the movie. For the rest of the night, Philip and I sat in disbelief as Dana and Ryan spent that time flirting with each other. I felt horrible for what I had put Philip through. I invited him over to help him, and the only help I provided was in getting his heart broken. I was upset too, but I couldn't figure out why. I figured I was just in a confusing place when it came to my friend Ryan. It was a great night indeed.

Our failed double date subsequently had Dana and me on the outs. I was stressed out because of the whole situation, and I had to play in chapel soon. The day just went from bad to worse. I did not play as well as I would have liked, and the tension between Dana and me was almost unbearable. With all the stress I was feeling, I finally had a kid day. I stopped trying to be everything else that everyone was trying to be—trying to fit in, trying to be popular, trying to get attention from boys. I was tired of it all. I finally acted like the fourteen-year-old that I was and played my Game Boy, worked on a crossword puzzle, and just enjoyed being who I was. I hoped that because of this all, I would never again try to be something I was not. This kid day of mine really helped because not too long afterward, a friend told me how Ryan seemed more comfortable with me than he did with Dana, and it just reaffirmed that I did not have to try to do anything—I just had to be me.

I had other things to focus on. As a sophomore, I could put in my application to be inducted into our chapter of the National Honor Society. It was a great honor, and not to mention, it would look great on my college applications—at least that was what everyone kept telling me. Lori, Gail, and I put in our applications. We could hardly wait to hear if we had made it in or not. The interviews and questions left us wondering if we did everything right. Finally, the day came, and we were informed of who made it in. Lorie was in—yes! I made it in—yes! Gail...did not. What? Wait, something was not right. We were all supposed to make it in. Why was Gail not in? She had the grades. Yeah, she may not have been in as many extracurricular activities as Lorie and I were, but that shouldn't have been held against her. Was it because she did not attend our church? She had her own home church. So what if it wasn't the same denomination. That shouldn't matter, right?

I found myself questioning everything I thought I knew. The whole situation had me doubting whether or not I wanted to be a part of a group that would deny such a great person. I was starting to think this was not what I wanted. I was only doing it because it was what I should have been doing and it would make everyone else happy; I knew I would not be. Well, one can only imagine how my parents were feeling at these words and thoughts. They implored my drama coach, who just happened to be the youth pastor's wife, to talk to me. After talking to her, I had to admit that I felt better. She let me know that I shouldn't be doing anything for other people or trying to please everyone. Ultimately, I should be trying to please God. It did make sense in theory, but by then, I had experienced so many emotional blows, talking to God was the last thing I wanted to do. I knew where my eternal soul would lie; I accepted Christ as my Savior when I was seven in the second grade. Needless to say the child that was so amazed with a big God had now turned into a passive and cynical observer who was fed up with trying so hard and getting nowhere.

Slowly, I found myself sinking deeper and deeper into a proverbial black hole. I stopped talking to my parents and kept holding everything in. The only outlet for the emotional torment going on inside me was poetry and writing. I wrote and I wrote and I wrote. I found I had lost my joy. I just wanted to be left alone. I had come to the conclusion that life just was not worth living. Everything I had hoped for and thought would make me happy had not. Ryan only saw me as a friend. I had joined the Honor Society only because it was what was expected of me, and my weight loss and increased involvement in activities had not helped much with my social plan. I had decided I would just kill myself because heaven would be an improvement to the life I had on earth. I found myself one day looking up at the trees and the sky and thinking how I would miss it all. I started to wonder how I would do it. A knife to the wrist was just too messy. I would just take some pills and drift off into a sleep I would never wake from.

My poetic words were getting darker, and one day I found myself in my room sitting on the floor in the dark. I was thinking of when I would go through with my newest plan. Somewhere in the dark, amid the screams that I had no worth and that no one loved me, I heard a still, small voice saying, "*I* love you." I was not hallucinating, and I knew that I was alone, so who could it be? I knew that in the depths of my soul, it was the very God who I wanted nothing to do with whispering to my wounded heart and soul. He was whispering to me in my self-loathing that He loved me and that He cared. It was as though a sliver of light was starting to peek through the dark shadow I had willingly allowed to be pulled over me. Over and over I was hearing the words *I love you* and that I had worth. The plans I had for my life up to that point obviously had not panned out, but God had a great plan for my life. He was not through with me yet. I could feel a warmth coming over me that was only growing and growing and the darkness had found that it had no place to hide.

By now, I was weeping like a baby on the floor in the middle of my room. God loved me! He cared! He had this great plan for my life, far exceeding anything I could think up for myself. I had grown up my whole life in a Christian home, going to church every Sunday and Wednesday, going to a Christian school, and that concept was only hitting me now. God really loved me. He sent his Son to die for my sins. I got that part when I was a kid, but in that moment of raw bitterness, anger, and hurt, God, in His infinite wisdom and mercy, saw fit to reach down and let me know He loved me. I felt as if I had just received a special gift from God. I was brought low to realize that when I thought I had nothing left, I had God and He was all I needed.

To say that my life was not forever changed by that one night would be a lie. I felt as if my eyes had been opened to so much. I was determined not to care anymore what others think of me. My plan for social supremacy didn't matter anymore. I was now on a quest to find out who I was.

The rest of the year flew by, and all that mattered before had little significance. Dana and I had since patched things up and performed a speech duet at fine arts. We did not place, and I was starting to wonder if acting was really for me. I was now facing my first piano recital in years, and I found again why I loved to play the piano in the first place. My piano teacher, Mrs. D., had reinvigorated my love for the instrument. She took my level of playing and brought it to a new level and even allowed me to experiment more with the type of pieces I enjoyed playing and not trying to force on me something that did not interest me. That time of year also brought about the spring play. I had decided to try out again, and this time, I got a part playing an old woman. I loved getting to know people I probably would never have talked to under normal circumstances, but I hated having to wash out the gray hair spray. I was learning to just enjoy each day as it came.

The previous summer, I had learned from Ryan that his family would be moving to their next post, and soon word came that they would be shipping off to Korea. Ryan had become a good friend, and my friendship with Angie had only grown, so much so we saw each other as sisters. I spent a lot of my days at their house and they were at mine. We became so close that we were the adopted children in each other's families. That was the kind of childhood you could only dream of. Yep, my best friends, the army brats, were being shipped to their next post, halfway around the world.

We were all crushed at the distance that would be between us and knew that the chances of us seeing each other again were slim. We decided we would have one last hurrah before they had to leave. Angie was going to be celebrating her thirteenth birthday and Ryan his sixteenth, their birthdays only being a day apart. It was the perfect time to have a party. Take a bunch of girls gathered for a slumber party and Ryan, combine some candy and caffeine, and one can only imagine how the night went.

We went through every emotion in that one night. At some point throughout the night, we each got a moment alone with Angie to share how much she meant to us and how much she would be missed. Needless to say, we came down after our respective turns with tears in our eyes. Early that morning, we found ourselves lying on the front lawn, staring up at the stars, in wonder of God and the creation He made. We were there long enough to watch the sun come up, and I was the last one to go in. After all I had been through, all I could do was sit in wonder at the creation all around me. To think, not too long ago I was thinking of saying good-bye to it all. We finally got to bed by seven o'clock, only to wake up at ten o'clock. Everyone was off to the skating rink, but I was getting ready to leave with my family for vacation. Having to say good-bye was the hardest thing for me to do. By the time we got back from our vacation, they were gone, and someone else was preparing to move into their house.

The summer progressed, and I found myself going on a whitewater rafting trip in which we also camped out in the middle of nowhere. The good thing about being out in the middle of nowhere was there were no lights and it was the perfect opportunity to see thousands of stars. Seeing those stars reminded me of the last night with Ryan and Angie, but it also reminded me of a God who loved me so much that He graciously reached down from heaven to break through my own darkness with His glorious light.

# CHAPTER THREE

*Do not go where the path may lead; go instead where there is no path and leave a trail.*
*—Ralph Waldo Emerson*

My junior year had begun. As usual, I tried out for the volleyball team, and I made it. My original reasons for wanting to participate in a sport were far different. Now, I played because I loved it. My outlook for that year was definitely different from that of the past two years. My eyes were starting to be opened to the hypocrisy around me. My class was ripping in two, and my church was in a stagnant state. It was hard hearing sermons and teachers tell you to live one way, knowing they were not doing the same. It was the "do as I say, not as I do" type of teaching—the very kind you do not listen to but end up having feelings of contempt and resentment for. I was starting to see that I spent too much time worrying about what others thought of me. I was going to spend less time worrying about them and more time focusing on me; easier said than done. I was spending too much time worrying, period. It was a daily struggle to let go of what I could not control and to just enjoy that moment that I was in.

I was still involved in all I was before—piano, yearbook, Honor Society, sports, the play—but this year, I was encouraged by my drama coach to do a speech by myself. I was already planning to do a duet with Chloe, despite the disaster the year prior with Dana, but doing one by myself? Being in front of people still scared me, even when I didn't have to say anything. But my coach had faith in me, was encouraging me, and thought that it was something I could do. I figured I would give it a try. What was the worst that could happen?

I was still battling issues with my self-perception. I felt that the beauty I had on the inside was not accurately being portrayed on the outside. I still felt that I just was not beautiful enough. I was still slim, but I was striving to be slimmer. Everything seemed to be wrapped up in what I looked like to others, and for some reason, that still mattered to me. I found it hard to just take a compliment without seeing something else behind it. It was always "thank you," but in my head I wondered what they meant by that exactly; talk about overanalyzing everything. I figured that one day, I would come to love the girl I saw reflecting back at me in the mirror. Until then, I was stuck with the half-like of myself. I just wanted the guys to stop seeing the outside, the color of my skin, and start to look at who I was on the inside. Beauty comes from within, right? Then why was I feeling that my beauty was contingent on the pigment on the outside?

In the meantime, my sixteenth birthday was approaching. I didn't have a huge party planned like most kids would want turning this significant age. In fact, I didn't even want a party. I was already bummed that Angie and Ryan couldn't be there to celebrate with me. It started off that morning with my mom calling in to my favorite Christian radio station and requesting "Butterfly Kisses" to be played for me. I was getting ready for school when the phone rang. In our family, the phone hardly ever rings before we leave for school, and if it does, it is some kind of emergency. My mom brought the phone to me, so I was assuming that it was one of my brothers calling to wish me a happy birthday. Much to my surprise and glee, it was Angie and Ryan calling from Korea to wish me a happy birthday. It was the best way to start the day.

I went on to receive flowers from my parents at school and be endlessly teased about it by my classmates; I didn't care. While I had no big extravaganza or fanfare to celebrate my sweet sixteen, all I received that day was truly priceless. Days later I received a package from Korea—my promised birthday gift from Angie and Ryan. Inside, I found a beautiful scroll that had my name artfully done in greens, oranges, and yellows. Also, I found a scrapbook that Angie made for me. It was documentation of her life from when she was small, to meeting me, and even what life was like for her in Korea. I sat in my room going through the pictures and drawings, knowing that even though they were thousands of miles away, I was very much loved.

With my birthday gone, that meant the yearly state fine arts competition was just around the corner. Chloe and I had practiced and practiced our duet. I, in turn, was putting the finishing touches on my speech, hoping I didn't get sick when it was my turn to perform. My coach gave me little tips to help me on the big day. I felt that I was ready. The day came and thankfully, Chloe and I would be doing our duet first. This was something I was familiar with, so the nerves were not as bad. Not to mention, there was someone else up in front of everyone with me. We got up to perform, and it was another complete disaster. Don't get me wrong; it was a funny speech and we got through it, but way too fast. By the time we were done, I just wanted to get out of there and get ready to face my next disaster.

As if I was not already nervous to perform solo, after the duet I was a bundle of nerves. To make matters worse, the girl in my school who was known to place really well in that category at these events was performing right before me, and it was a packed room; no pressure. It was finally my turn. My hands were sweating, and I was praying I could get through it and remember all my lines. My speech was about four women in a beauty parlor discussing all the latest gossip a bit too loudly. I got through the performance, and thankfully, people laughed when they were supposed to. I had my family and friends present to support me, so no matter what happened at the awards ceremony, I knew I did my best. I left knowing I would be happy with an excellent rating.

We (by we, I mean all present to represent my school and all other schools and family members) all piled into the auditorium for the closing ceremonies. I did not hold out much hope for Chloe and me placing, so by the time they got to the awards for the speech category, I had almost zoned out. They got to the humorous interpretation category, and the girl from my school placed third. We all clapped politely, knowing that deep down inside we were wishing she could have gotten first place. They got to second place, and it sounded like they said my name. By the looks of surprise on the faces around me and the applause, I realized they did. I stood up in utter disbelief to acknowledge the crowd and sat right back down because it could not be happening. I got second place? Really? Hey, maybe I was good at this after all!

The excitement of fine arts died down and we were all getting ready for Junior/Senior. It was our private school version of prom. As always, the juniors planned the event for the seniors. We brainstormed over the how, where, and what and surprisingly came to a consensus decision. Most junior classes held it somewhere on school property, but we wanted to be different. Also, we figured if we did a great job on this, it was only fair that next year, the juniors would do a great job for us. The day came, and we got to leave school early, not to get dressed, but to finish decorating. We built the set the night before and decorated as much of the inside as we could. It was during that time that I discovered that racism was still alive and kicking in my class. There was a group of guys who were known as the "rednecks" of the school. They were proud of their heritage and showed it by display-ing the confederate flag anywhere they could. There were times they would wave it in my face, hoping to get a reac-tion out of me. What they failed to realize was that the South was not my heritage and I couldn't have cared less what a flag from that time period meant. That evening we were painting the lattice black for the back drop of our theme. It was then that one of the guys decided to come up to me and tell me he wanted to paint me. I was furious. I told him to leave me alone, but he persisted to say how it would match. It was then that our sponsor saw that I was upset and found out what was going on. She took care of the situation. Their antics were something we had put up with for years and were finally getting tired of. The odd thing was that the night prior I had a dream (or rather a nightmare) in which I was telling that very guy off. Despite what happened the night before, I was determined not to let them get the best of me. We had a wonderful menu of Caesar salad, filet mignon, and twice-baked potatoes. We got a great photographer, and our theme, Magic of the Millennium, was engraved on everyone's glass, which they got to take home with them.

Everything was perfect—except my dress. My aunt, a professional seamstress, made my dress for me, but she was unable to find the color fabric that I wanted. It was still beautiful, but I built up my expectation too high. I was off to the mall to have my makeup done, and I should have known something would go wrong by the look of the makeup on the lady's face. Word of advice: If you are ever getting your makeup done for you, take a close look at the makeup of the person who is doing it. If it looks crazy and out of your taste, chances are you will end up looking the same way. Sadly, I did. Now I was grumpy because I looked like a caked-on, blue-eyed Smurf, and I was late meeting up with my friends. I had to resort to my parents dropping me off (yeah, I didn't have a date). It was not a good way to start the night. Eventually, I cooled off and enjoyed the rest of the evening. We laughed and relaxed for a glamorous night to end the year. I made friends with some of the people in the senior class over the year in some of the most unusual ways. There were bus trips to games, the youth ski trip, the school play, and classes. By the time graduation came around, I was truly sad to see them go. I knew that this time next year, it would be my turn and frankly, the thought was scary.

My summer was jam-packed. The new thing for me that summer was going on a mission trip. I wanted to go mainly because the year before, they went to Mexico and I felt left out when they came back sharing the stories of their adventures. I still wanted to fit in. Old habits die hard. That summer we were going to be traveling around the South, mainly Georgia, South Carolina, and Florida. We would be visiting churches with a music and drama team. Thankfully I didn't need to raise too much money as we were staying with people from the various churches we would be visiting. At one of the churches, we would be staying in their gym. Since I did not think of myself as much of a singer, I tried out for the drama team. Two weeks on the road would be long enough to be away from home, but I knew it would be a great experience; it was too. I was able to learn so much and do so much. I had the privilege of meeting great and kind people that I would not have had the chance to otherwise. I even found some friendships in places I never would have imagined. I was able to make memories that would stay with me forever.

I of course went on another whitewater rafting trip. Last year's was scary, but it was the most fun I had ever had. I remembered coming around the river thinking, *What have I gotten myself into?* But by the time it was done, I found myself wondering when the next trip would be. This year, I could hardly wait to get in the raft. The excitement faded when I realized that the rapids on this river were much calmer than the previous year's river, and we were pretty much just rowing downriver, goofing off. Don't ask me why, but Chloe and I got in a raft with our youth pastor. He was on a mission to knock everyone in our boat out. I made it downriver, nearly to the end of the trip, without being thrown out. Unfortunately, we stopped on the side, waiting for other boats to catch up, and I let my guard down. Next thing I knew, I was being thrown overboard. Another thing I had been afraid of in my life was water. It took me three years as a kid to finally learn how to swim and even now, they cannot pay me to go into the deep end of the pool. You can only imagine what it was like going headfirst into water I couldn't even see in that was about forty degrees or so. I came up gasping for air and praying that the boat I saw coming my way didn't go over my head. I was finally pulled back into the boat, and all I could say to my youth pastor was, "What? Are you trying to kill me?" Everyone had a good laugh (even me, eventually), but for the rest of the summer, every time my youth pastor saw me, he just looked at me, made his eyes go really big, and opened his mouth wide in an attempt to mimic my entry into the water.

That summer I learned so much about myself, but mainly I learned that people were not always what you thought they were. Sometimes, you could find yourself pleasantly surprised.

# CHAPTER FOUR

*Never tell a young person that anything cannot be done. God may have been waiting centuries for someone ignorant enough of the impossible to do that very thing.*

—*John Andrew Holmes*

It was the start of my senior year, and I was facing it with mixed emotions. On one hand, I, like everyone else, could not wait to get out of there and to be free from some of the ridiculous rules. On the other hand, I was rather apprehensive of leaving the comfort of the place I had known for the last ten years. Since it was my last year, I decided that I was going to be involved in everything I could be. My day generally went like this:

6:00 a.m.—Wake up and get ready for school.

7:15 a.m.—Had to leave the house by this time to get to school by 7:30 for any meetings (Honor Society namely)

8:00 a.m. to 3:10 p.m.—Classes

3:30 p.m.—Practice started, and that year, I also was trying out for the basketball team. Come spring, this was also play practice.

5:30 p.m.—Practice ended (play practice could have gone longer), and I headed home. I got a shower and grabbed a quick bite to eat.

6:30 p.m.—I started my homework and would not stop sometimes until 1:00 a.m.—depending on how tough the Calculus problems were.

I eventually fell into bed and got up at six o'clock the next morning to start all over again. And I even managed to maintain a social life. If only my goals were the same as back when I was a freshman…

My core group of friends had increased from just the girls I hung out with in my class. Now, I was hanging out with Jane, Sabrina, and Tabby. Jane was the first friend I made when I got to South Carolina. She was this short blonde kid who stuck up for me when I was incessantly picked on by a girl in my class. She was my protector, and I loved her for it. Over the years, she turned into a blonde knockout that all the guys wanted to date. Sabrina was a quiet brunette beauty who knew how to make me laugh. She was teased for being quiet, namely because there was always talk of what really lay underneath—an adventurous soul just waiting to bust loose. Most of the times when we all hung out in a group with Robert, Peter, and Luke, it was at Sabrina's house. Of course, Tabby was still Tabby and in a way, I saw her as my guardian angel because she was always looking out for my well-being.

Luke had been around the longest. He had dark hair, and his eyes were so closed, you sometimes wonder if he was squinting. Robert and Peter showed up to the school around the same time, their tenth-grade year. Robert was rather pale, with blonde hair, but had a great sense of humor. Peter was probably the hunkiest of the three—tall, with light brown hair, and could have been a model in another life. Unfortunately, as one of my friends once said, he was cute until he opened his mouth to say something. He had a rather thick southern accent. Over the years he had been there, it grew on us so his cuteness had been reinstated.

In my returning for the school year, I learned that Will was going to be one of my teachers. Will and I went way back. When I was in elementary, he was in high school and his after-school job was working in the daycare. With my mom working for the school, that was where I ended up until she got off work. It did not take long for Will and I to develop a friendship—one that included nicknames. He affectionately called me "Buckwheat" because sometimes my hair would stand up like his. I called him "Spanky" because he was shaped like him. Since then, every time we saw each other, those were the names we used. Flash forward to my senior year and I was supposed to call him mister? Yeah, I opted for calling him "Coach," as he was also the coach of the guys' basketball team.

That year my drama coach decided I needed to get a jump on things and decided that I needed to enroll for the annual BJ Festival. This was a competition held for high school students on the campus of Bob Jones University.

I was a little apprehensive about this, for the sole reason that my beliefs on interracial dating did not add up with the previous beliefs of the school. Up until my sophomore year of high school, BJ had a rule against interracial dating. Bradley's wife had spent a semester or two at the school, and she had roommate that was from the Philippines. They told her that she looked white enough so she could date the white guys. After hearing this story and knowing their previous beliefs, it was hard for me to go to a school, even to visit, that seemed so racists. My parents raised me to love everyone. There was not a clause put on love because of the color of someone's skin. Love everyone meant just that. I went anyway because my friends were going and it was a few days away from school. While they did not have a category for my speech, I did get good reviews. I was hopeful for that year's fine arts competition. After my previous year's success, I was gunning for first place. I gained confidence in myself in that area, and I felt I had found my niche. Yes, it took me three years, but I still found it. That was what counted.

I still struggled with my weight and just being accepted as a whole. My emotions were a constant roller coaster ride that I could only pray would come to a stop. Most days I was content with life and the hand I had been dealt, and then there were the days when I could not wait for graduation day to be upon us so I could hopefully put it all behind me. I started to resent being black in a white school—I felt as though that was my one problem, and I knew there was nothing I could do to fix it.

Since it was my senior year, it was only logical to be thinking of colleges. To that point, I had no idea what I wanted to major in. Those in my class going to college knew and were ready, and I felt a little behind in the scheme of things. I was getting information from schools all over the country, and I had no idea what a treasure trove I had before me. I heard from the University of Southern California, UGA, Wake Forest, and North Carolina State just to name a few. At the time, that didn't mean a thing to me. See, my school only promoted other Christian schools that they approved of, and that was a short list. I could choose from Bob Jones, Pensacola, Crown, or Ambassador. None of these were really to my liking so I just figured I would attend the University of South Carolina and be done with it.

While this was going on, I was still involved in my favorite sport—volleyball. There was a new coach, and things were going well, until she injured her foot and we found ourselves temporarily without a coach. We had to rally around ourselves and find the strength deep within to continue on in the season. While we didn't go on to state that year, it was by far my best year of playing. The last game I played was a good moment tinged with sadness. We lost to our rivals, and I had to come to grips with the fact that it was the last time I would put on my number three jersey. The upside was that my family was present for every single game to cheer me on and give their support.

One sport out and another sport in—basketball season began, and by some miracle, I made the team. I was only trying out to be involved, so riding the pine most of the season was no skin off my back. There were a few times that I got to play, and I even scored some easy baskets. Of course, the one thing that really stuck out in my head was one game where we were warming up and unfortunately, the guys' team just had to be sitting in the stands, watching. We were doing our lay-up drills. When my turn came, I found that somehow the line I was standing in had moved up so far, I was already right under the basket. There was nothing for me to do but pass the ball. Unfortunately, Coach Will saw the whole thing. I got ragged about it for a week or so. Can you feel the love? The season flew by in a rush and our last game was upon us. It was a bittersweet moment as we lost to our rivals, and while I realized it was the last time I would put on my jersey, it was also a relief because I honestly did not enjoy playing basketball like I had volleyball.

Winter turned to spring and with basketball season firmly behind me, I prepared for fine arts and also the spring play. I was more active in fine arts that I had been in previous years. I was in the school choir and had my own speech and a chorale reading with other speech students. It may not seem like much, but for me, it was enough to keep me busy. My main focus was my own personal speech. My friends loved it, and my mom couldn't get enough. They were all doing wonders for my ego. This speech was different from the last in that I had a German accent, and I was only really doing one voice. I was excited to perform. The nerves were present on the big day, but they had turned into excited nerves. I went in and did my thing. When I was finished, I was proud of my efforts, and I was really hopeful of taking first. Upon entering the auditorium for the award's ceremony, however, I knew that it was not to be so.

Every year, they chose a few of the first place winners to perform in various areas as part of the showcase. That year my category was among those picked, but my name was not on the list. I soon found out that I took second place for the second time in as many years. This time, the emotion I was feeling was disappointment. I would get some retribution as I got to perform for my school's showcase of those who placed at fine arts. My friends went on that night to encourage me and help me along in my performance (not that I was nervous, but rather because they were sitting off to the right of the stage). That night was my best performance because I knew the crowd that I was performing in front of really appreciated it.

Upon returning from fine arts, I was faced with finishing out the rest of the semester. I still had no idea what I was going to major in when I got to college. Our English teacher had us write word papers; papers that were written on a simple word like love or faith. For one of my papers, I received the word *hope*. I put a lot into that paper. It turned out to be one of the best papers I had ever written to date. However, it was not the grade that I got for the paper that got me. It was rather the meaning of the single word—*hope*. There was so much power in it that I realized that I wanted nothing more than to be able to bring hope into the lives of those I encountered.

What better way to do that than as a doctor? I was finally starting to feel as if I knew what my purpose was in life.

With one major decision out of the way, there came the decision of what school to attend. There was a trip coming up for Pensacola Christian College (PCC for short), and since I had never been there and it was free, I figured who would I be to pass up a free trip to Florida during school? Also, I saw the trip as my first step to independence. Since none of my girlfriends were going, it was the perfect time to start trying to do things for myself. To make it even better, my friends Peter, Luke, and Robert were going. For the first time, I had the guys all to myself. I was going to enjoy it while it lasted. It didn't make much of a difference that Dad was the one driving the bus because I was the center of attention. It was hard to be noticed when you had other girlfriends who outshine you most of the time. I had a great time and during those few days, I got to know the guys a little bit better. Between the fact that it was a ten-hour trip and none of the girls were around to monopolize any-one's time or attention, I felt pretty special. I enjoyed myself, and I also quickly discovered that PCC was not the school for me.

The next events to follow were Junior/Senior (which I, of course, had no date for again), the spring play (in which I played an old woman again), my final piano recital, and the senior trip. Each year, the seniors took a trip to New York and Washington, D.C. Our class always joked our trip would involve walking across the street to the chapel and watching film footage of previous classes on their senior trips. I say this for the simple reason that our class did not have the best reputation. Since my coming in the second grade, we always made a teacher cry; we even got one to retire. In junior high, they coincidentally started a new discipline system just as we arrived. Teachers dreaded the thought of having us as a class. Our reputation preceded us. I would never forget being a freshman and overhearing a teacher state: "I have just given up on that class." It broke my heart to hear those words.

It didn't help that the class above us was, by all accounts, the "perfect" class. They got all the praise and preferential treatment, and when it came our turn, we got the short end of the stick. It was no wonder that our class motto as seniors was "We got shafted." Thankfully though, they did take us on our trip, and boy, it was interesting. I had been to both places before at least once by then, so not much was new for me. For others, it was seemingly the first time out of the state. There was the mooing in the Holland Tunnel, ridiculous spending on Fifth Avenue, losing people in Time Square, and the offers to go up for tapings of shows for MTV. There were the trips to FAO Schwartz, Trump Towers, Saint Patrick's Cathedral, the Statue of Liberty, and the Twin Towers. (I even took some pictures at the window. I was terrified up there.) We even visited Little Italy and Chinatown. I was pleasantly surprised to find us having a good time and actually enjoying each other's company. Another joke that prevailed was that half of us would end up in jail for killing the other half (maybe that one was mine). We left for DC, and the fun continued for the rest of the week making great memories.

By the time we got back, we knew there were only a few weeks left until we reached the day we worked so hard for. That day would come sooner than we knew it, and it would be the end and the beginning. Finals week was upon me before I knew it, and I was starting to wonder where I ranked in the class. The day before my final and only exam—calculus—I was told that it would be between Lorie and me for salutatorian. Gail had already secured the position of valedictorian. Evidently, everyone but me knew this fact, and our calculus exam was going to be the deciding factor. I already had enough pressure on me just to do well on the exam, but now I knew I had to nail it.

Those of us that had the pleasure of taking calculus struggled all year simply because there were not enough hours in the school day and the teacher had to teach both senior math classes in one class period. Most days, she would start off teaching the other class leaving the rest of us barely enough time to get through that day's lesson. We would end up having to practically teach ourselves. I had to get a SparkNotes book on calculus to help me understand the parts I just couldn't get a grasp on. I wasn't sure how I was going to make it through finals. The day came, and I nervously worked my way through the final. I left the room knowing that I did my best and I tried my hardest. Now it was just a waiting game. Before the day came to an end, we knew the results; I did it! I would be the salutatorian, and that meant I had only a couple of days to write my speech. I was able to get a hold of previous salutatorian speeches, and I worked from there. About half an hour later, I had my speech. When I found out that Gail took a few hours to write hers, I felt maybe that I should do it again. But after reading through my speech again, I knew it said all that I wanted it to say and I did not need to change a thing.

Graduation finally came and with it all the anticipation and excitement that had been building up. This was going to be the happiest day of my life to date. I mean, my class was going to be the first class to graduate in the newly built auditorium; nothing could go wrong. Boy, was I wrong. Remember I said that I was not considering too many colleges and I was just going to go to the University of South Carolina? Unfortunately, there were those who did not think that this was a great idea. How would a girl who had gone to private school all of her life fare at a public university? "Not well" apparently seemed to be the consensus thinking. My youth pastor had convinced my father that it was a big mistake and that I was meant to go to PCC.

The morning of my graduation, I found myself sitting in the pastor's office with my mom, dad, and Leah. Dad had brought me there in hopes of talking some sense into me. By now, what was supposed to be a happy occasion had turned into a complete nightmare. On top of that, I found out that not all of my brothers were going to make it for my graduation. By the time we left the pastor's office, I was on the verge of angry tears. I thought this was supposed to be my decision, not one forced on me. I finally conceded and told the principal that when I walked across the stage, he was to announce that I would attend PCC in the fall. Thankfully and mercifully, he stated that I was undecided about my college plans. Well that was just one bullet dodged for now.

At the reception, I affectionately greeted Coach Will as Spanky for the first time that year. The drama of earlier in the day drained away as my friends and family headed back to our house for a party. The future looked bright, right? I was starting a new chapter in my life. There were many clichés you could probably think of to apply to this momentous occasion, but frankly, all I felt was fear and dread. I had no idea where I was going, and I was starting to feel like tumbleweed in the desert looking for a safe place to land. There was a lot weighing on my seventeen-year-old shoulders. All I could think was *God, help me*; I really needed it.

S ummer began, and with it came a few new things for me. I was getting my driver's license, and I had my very first date. Yeah, I know—a little crazy for both, but I only turned seventeen two months prior, so it was not all that bad. I had had my permit since I was fifteen, but there was no need to get my license. My parents drove me to school because we were all going to the same place, and I rode with my friends if we went out somewhere. I will admit that finally having my license gave me a new sense of freedom. My date was not one of those memorable first dates you read about or see in the movies. It started earlier than planned. I was sick, and I came home early knowing it was also the last date with that guy.

I also signed up for another mission trip. This time it was a ten-day trip to Puerto Rico to help some missionaries our church had down there. By the time the trip came around though, I was having second thoughts. Frankly, I did not want to go. I stalled as much as I possibly could, but I eventually found myself on a plane with my youth group and by the way some of them were acting, I had to think it was their first time on a plane. Four hours later, we were in San Juan and the trip had officially started. This time, I was more behind the scenes and only singing when it was a big group. During the day, we were helping to clear out their property and make repairs in some of the buildings. In the afternoon, we went out to invite kids in the neighborhood to join us for vacation bible school. At night, we held the VBS services and got a chance to unwind after a long day.

During one of the days, I found myself in a room with several other people as we painted the walls and the trim. It was at this time that my youth pastor found it appropriate to tell me that I was making a big mistake by not going to college right away and that to delay it for a guy was ridiculous. After all the drama he helped cause on graduation, I could not help but wonder who this guy thought I was. If he knew me at all, he would first of all know how important college was to me so no matter what, I was going. Secondly, no guy could stop me from doing what I knew God had for me to do. I was not one of those guy-crazy girls in high school whose life revolved around who she was dating that particular week or who she would date the following week. I had my crushes, but that was as far as they went. I had long since come to accept that while the guys may have found me attractive, it seemed those who wanted to possibly do something about it were just too afraid of what other people would think. I silently took in all he was saying, but the only thing it was doing for me was giving me the resolve to prove him wrong.

The week progressed just fine with the occasional free time trips to the beach, Old San Juan, and El Yunique, the rainforest on the island. I was having a good enough time, but I was just not as into the experience as I should have been; that all changed on one of the last nights of VBS. After every service, there was an invitation, and it was our responsibility to pray with any child that came forward. On that night, I was fortunate enough to pray with a young girl, no more than seven or eight. The words she spoke to me after we prayed will stay with me and echo through my mind. She looked me dead in the eyes and with such joy on her face, she said to me, "Thank you for saving my life." I really didn't do anything, but her words struck a chord in my heart. In that moment, I realized that life was so much more than just vacations, school, family, or friends. It was about people—those we encounter every day who do not know Christ. It was about the light we were to shine that represents Christ in our lives. I knew that I was forever changed and my perception of people was totally different from when I began the trip. I would discover rather quickly in the months to come just how important this all was.

# CHAPTER FIVE

*Why is it that when we talk to God we're said to be praying, but when God talks to us we're schizophrenic?*
—*Lily Tomlin*

The new school year was upon us, and most of my classmates were getting ready to be freshmen in a few weeks. I still felt a little lost, but for a few hours, I was going to just forget it and return to the school with Mom and Leah for open house. It was so nice knowing that it was not for me, and I was relishing the moment. We spent the earlier part of the afternoon running errands, and we were heading home to get ready for the night. When we got home, we found a message on our answering machine that changed everything. Mom pressed play, and all I heard was a scream and watched her collapse on the floor in a heap. She was crying. I couldn't understand what she was trying to tell me, but I knew it wasn't good. I replayed the message that had caused her to go limp, and in an instant, I knew why. One of our cousins had called to inform us that my cousin Trey was dead. The news hit like a load of bricks. I took it particularly hard because he was the only cousin I had that was close to my age. We used to play together as kids; now he was gone. Everything else happened on cruise control. I collected Mom off the floor and told her we had to get dressed and head to the school for Leah. We still had things that needed to get done. It was a rather subdued time at open house. So many questions came to mind, like how did this happen and what went wrong, and it made it difficult to process the news. We were also wondering how his family was taking the shocking news. We got back in record time, and Mom was making the necessary calls to family in St. Lucia to find out what happened. Trey and two of his friends were in Canada for a music festival. His friend was driving and his friend's girlfriend and Trey had fallen asleep. Apparently, the guy drifted off to sleep himself. Next thing they were in an accident that found both Trey and the girlfriend dead. They assumed they went quietly in their sleep, not knowing what happened.

We found ourselves in a whirlwind because the funeral was coming up and we needed to get to St. Lucia. Since it was a death in the family, Dad was able to get Mom, Leah, and I last minute tickets for the weekend. Leah was going to be spending her tenth birthday in airports and on planes. We were just hoping that we made it in time for the funeral. Three planes and two layovers later, we arrived exhausted. We arrived at the place we were staying and fortunately, it was right across the street from Trey's mother's house. We got some rest, and that night, they had a wake that was doubling as a family reunion. Leah and I were meeting people we had never seen in our lives and getting to see people we had not seen in years. My aunt, who was also Trey's grandmother, had come in from London. This was the first time in years that my mom and her two sisters were together in the same place.

The day of the funeral arrived, and I was not looking forward to it. I guess that was kind of silly to think, because who looks forward to a funeral? Funerals just remind me of my own mortality and how it just as easily could have been me. We got to the funeral home and my other aunt broke down. I could barely bring myself to the casket after that. He was so young. The encouraging thing in all of this was that so many around the island spoke so highly of him. Apparently Trey became a Christian before his death and many spoke of his witness to them. That brought a smile to my face on such a glum day. If he was making such an impact, what more could I be doing to have the same said of me if I were the one lying there?

By the time we got to the church, there was a crowd outside. With both of his parents being involved in the government, it brought a slow halt to the island. The service was somber and beautiful. I could tell that my cousin was deeply loved. The procession to the gravesite was long, and by the time we got there, I realized I had not cried yet that entire time. That, however, was to be quickly remedied. As I watched them lower Trey's coffin into the ground, it hit me. The tears which had yet to fall were now coming in buckets, and Mom could do little to console me. Trey was not coming back. He was truly gone.

The rest of our time there we enjoyed the company of our relatives. Even with the sad reason for our being there, it was good for Mom to have her sisters around. I had not seen her so happy in a long time. It had been a while since she was home, and it had been years since I was there; for Leah, it was a first. By the time we were on our way home, we had the opportunity to see the volcano, visit Sulfur Springs, see the Pitons, and make many great memories. On the plane ride home, I had no idea what our country was about to face in just a few weeks.

Everyone remembers what they were doing on September 11 when the planes hit the towers. I was just getting up and, in my sleepy state, thought the footage I was seeing was from a previous time the Twin Towers had been hit. It did not take long to realize that what I was watching was live. The phones in the house were not working, so I had to run to a neighbor's to use their phone. I just wanted to hear someone's voice from my family. The rest of the day went by in slow motion as we waited to hear from relatives living in New York City. Sitting at work, I found it hard to concentrate, wondering if more strikes were to come.

In the days following 9/11, getting back to life as normal was a little difficult. Eventually, I found myself faced with the decision of what college to go to. Still feeling a little pressure from Dad, I didn't have a clue what to do. I was asking God for help because I knew that ultimately, He would lead me where I was supposed to go. I applied to the University of South Carolina Honors College, only to be told I had to wait a year because they were already full. I wanted to apply to Duke, but the deadline had passed and that would mean waiting a year; I was running out of options.

By now, it was January, and a freak snow storm had hit. That gave me a few days off of work, and I used this time to earnestly seek God. The snow was coming down lightly, and I looked out the window, crying out to God for help. I asked for a sign, a sign to let me know it would all work out. I asked for a simple shift in the wind, and before the words were completely out of my mouth, the wind had picked up and it was now snowing at an angle. Some can say it was just a coincidence, but I do not believe in coincidences. I felt a peace fall over me, knowing that my God was going to take care of me.

I went back to a collection of college information I had accumulated, and I started to shift through the pile. It was only then that I noticed the brochure from Liberty University. I had been to the campus before for a friend of the family's graduation, but that was a while back. I didn't remember much, but I knew it was a Christian university that was out in the middle of nowhere; there was not much around when we were there. I noticed that the brochure said that some of the nursing students had gone on to work at Duke; this got my attention. (Did I mention that I am a *huge* Duke Blue Devils fan?)

I started to pray, and eventually, I brought the brochure for Dad to see and read. I needed him to understand that no matter where I went to school, it had to be my decision and for the right reason. That year off of school had taught me that I needed to stand on *my own faith* and I needed the room to be able to do that. After reading the information and praying about it himself, he realized he had been wrong and if I felt that Liberty was where God was leading me, he was okay with it; talk about a load off my shoulders!

I applied for Liberty in the spring, and the day I received my acceptance letter was one of the best days in my life. I was relieved to find out that Luke would also be attending Liberty in the fall so I would not be completely alone. I had to get ready for college, and while I was excited, I was also nervous at having to move away. But I was ready for a change of scenery. The life I had in South Carolina was growing stale, and I was starting to see that my school and church were not as perfect as I once thought. Many of the people I graduated with had strayed from what they were taught. Some had stopped going to church; some had turned to alcohol and smoking, and some had found themselves with children on the way. In our own ways, we had all realized that while we were being taught to live and act in school and church one way, many of those same people were not practicing what they preached. The hypocrisy was enough to turn many away from what they learned their entire lives. I was determined to find out what being a Christian was truly all about. My parents had set a good example for me and while they were not perfect, I knew they had done their best. It was now my turn to set my own course. God would surely have something great for me at Liberty.

# CHAPTER SIX

*Other people may be there to help us, teach us, guide us along our path. But the lesson to be learned is always ours.*

—*Melody Beattie*

I found myself getting ready for my freshman year in a bit of a frazzled mode. Two weeks before we were to leave for Lynchburg, I was sitting in the dentist's office being told my wisdom teeth needed to come out. They could perform the procedure that week or I could wait until Christmas break, but my wisdom teeth had no room to grow, so there was no telling what amount of pain I could be in by then. All I could think was that I was not in any pain at all right at the moment! Reluctantly, I agreed. That was a mistake. Something that was supposed to be routine had turned into a complete disaster.

While at the dentist, I had some cavities filled. Unfortunately during that time, my jaw locked up and put me in horrible pain. Eventually they massaged it down, but by then, I was terrified of my upcoming wisdom teeth removal. Luckily, I had been told that I would be put to sleep because they had to cut into my gums to get the teeth out. I went in the following week and came out in a daze, not really remembering how I got home. The rest of the day proved to be nothing but a big haze for me. I was not in much pain, if any, but I was still fuzzy and not walking well. The dentist told me that the effects were to wear off in a day or so, but four days later, I was still feeling the effects. It was time for me to leave for school, but I was in no shape to go anywhere. By now, Dad had a virus, and it looked like I had a viral infection; so much for freshman orientation.

When we finally left, I was starting to second-guess myself. Maybe this wasn't such a good idea; maybe I was wrong. However, when we got to campus, I could just tell that there was something different about this place. I just knew that the years I was to spend there would be truly blessed and unlike anything I had experienced thus far in my life. I could possibly find the answers to my questions here. Because we left late, I was arriving when the returning students were showing up and there was no room for me on campus. I was temporarily put in Dorm 2, living with the spiritual life directors (SLDs for short). It was not the way I pictured my college life beginning.

The girls on the dorm were rather unique. I had already met two, Alex and Darcy, and they had me thinking this was the place for me. Alex was a short firecracker. With her curly brown hair and five foot two small frame, she brought a smile to my face with her antics. Darcy was a little taller and had dark hair and had the wit to match Alex. I also met Beth, who was about my height, with blonde hair and a dry sense of humor that I loved. While I bonded with all of the girls on the hall, those three became my close friends. Unfortunately, I was only living on the hall temporarily until they could find me a room. I found myself shortly moving to what felt like the other side of campus and rooming with two other freshmen. They were great and as sweet as could be, but I formed a bond and attachment with the other dorm and even their brother dorm (equivalent of fraternity). I found myself just biding my time until a bed opened up for me to move back. In only a few weeks' time, I found myself back "home"—right where I belonged—on Dorm 2. It was as if I had never left.

Adjusting to dorm and college life did not take long, and before I knew it, I found myself in a routine. I went to class, came back for a nap before dinner, and then headed out with my friends for the evening. It was normally Alex, Darcy, Beth, and me as well as Tom and Mike and occasionally a few other random guys from their dorm. Tom could be described as a Christopher Gorham with light brown curly hair and facial hair. Without the facial hair, he looked about six years younger than he really was. Mike was a dark-haired standout who played the guitar and loved music. By standout, I mean a little off center, but for some reason, I found myself attracted to him. I had found my family away from home.

That first semester, death had hit our hall in waves. Darcy had only just started seeing a guy only to get a phone call early one morning to inform her that he was tragically killed in a car accident. You never forget the cry of agony when someone gets news like that. We gathered around her to give her as much support as we could. We knew that God was in control, but the pain was still there. Alex ended up going with her to the funeral to be a support system.

Not two weeks had passed, and it was my turn to experience the pain. It was a Saturday, and I was just getting back from dinner with everyone when one of my roommates told me that my phone had been ringing. I always forgot to take it with me. I picked it up to learn I had missed three calls. One was from my brother, Jack, asking if I was okay; the other two were from my parents asking me to give them a call. By the tone of their voices, I knew that something was wrong. I called home immediately to find out what was going on, fearing that it had something to do with Leah. She had open-heart surgery when she was four to repair a hole in her heart; not too long after that, she started experiencing seizures. She had grown out of them, and everything seemed to be okay. Now I was wondering if that was not the case.

When I got a hold of my mom, she kept asking me if I was sitting down and if there was anyone there with me. I just wanted her to tell me what was wrong. Finally, she told me that Will was dead.

I knew I let out my own groan as my knees found the ground because my roommates were surrounding me.

Before long, Darcy, Alex, and Beth were there with the RAs and SLDs. All I could do was listen as Mom told me the details of how Will had been found and that he had taken his own life. I could not help but flash back to the time when I had wanted to do the same thing. I was sick. I wanted so badly to go home for the funeral, but it was in the middle of the week, and Mom and Dad were worried about the classes I would miss. Tom offered to take me home for the funeral, but I eventually realized that my parents were right. Instead, I did not go to classes that day, explaining to my professors what had happened; they thankfully understood the whole situation. I needed the time to grieve. No longer would it be Spanky and Buckwheat, and it hurt more than I could say. If I was taking it so hard, I could only imagine how everyone at home was taking it. My heart went out to his family. That October proved to be a very dark one.

I made it through midterms and Thanksgiving, and I only had finals to go. My first semester as a frosh was coming to an end, but not before open dorms. Open dorms were the yearly event that took place during Christmas when the guys got to come in the girls' dorms and vice versa. I sat and watched as people around me decorated their rooms and doors with Christmas decorations in great anticipation. My roommates were not too into open dorms, so our decorations were minimal at best. I did not mind much, and I was getting into the spirit of things in other people's rooms. It was going to be a great night. It was too, until we made our way to the guys' dorm. Alex and I were visiting some friends, but between having a spat with the guys and someone pulling the fire alarm, we found ourselves sitting at Dairy Queen enjoying ice cream as we discussed how crummy guys were.

Alex and I discovered we were in a class together so it made passing the time a little less unbearable. It was one of those classes that you had right after lunch and you could feel the sleep coma coming on. Considering that the room was freezing cold all the time, one would think that would not happen; not so. During one class in particular, Alex and I looked back at the back row of students to see every single one of them fast asleep. That class was supposed to be one of the tougher general classes you would have to take at LU, but Alex and I studied and were doing surprisingly well considering all we had heard about it. The time for the final approached and we studied as hard and as long as we could. We went in for the final, feeling pretty good about ourselves. If we could get past this, the start of exams would be behind us and maybe the rest of our finals would not seem so bad. Fifteen minutes after starting the exam, Alex and I were on our way back to the dorm. We could not believe how easy the final was and were starting to wonder what all the hype was about that class. That day I learned to take what people said about certain classes with a grain of salt.

By the time the semester ended, I found myself sad to go and eager to get back to start the second semester. That semester held so many firsts for me—my first concert, my first college road trip, and my first college crush. I could only imagine what the next semester held for me.

I t was now my second semester, and I felt like an old pro. I had the advantage on the new freshman coming in for this semester, and it made me feel experienced. My friendships were growing, especially my friendship with Tom. We were so close that we knew when the other person was either lying or leaving something out of the conversation. The friendship I had with Mike had deteriorated, and not just with me. He turned more jerk-like toward us all and we blamed it on the new girl in his life. I was just excited that he had invited me to the Valentine's Day banquet. I was all dressed up and my friends were saying how great I looked. My hopes were dashed when I got to the car and found the new girl already in the car; so much for my crush. Where was Tom when I needed him? By the time we got back from the banquet, my mood had turned to gloomy. Luckily, Alex was there to help lighten the mood. We headed off to the Valentine's Day coffeehouse with Tom, and the day ended much better than it started. Those two were quickly becoming the people I could depend on and trust. I would need it soon.

My nineteenth birthday was approaching, and I must say that Tom and Mike helped influence my music taste that year. When I learned that my favorite band, Switchfoot, was holding a concert back home the weekend of my birthday, I knew that meant one thing—road trip! Alex, her boyfriend, Joe, Tom, and I piled in Tom's car and headed home. It was the best concert that I had been to, and when it was over, Tom was determined to get his copies of their CDs autographed. I had their latest CD with me, but being the shy one that I am, I just wanted to head home because I didn't think we stood a chance of actually meeting anyone. Tom was persistent. He brought me back inside, and it just so happened that the lead singer was coming back out to mingle with the people that were there. Tom stopped him and we started to talk. He was so kind and autographed our CDs for us. It is still one of my most prized possessions. I found that Tom had given me one of the best birthday presents.

It was not long in our returning back to school that I got the news from home that my grandmother was sick. Evidently, she had been for a while and just had not told anyone. It was spring break, and unlike most kids who were at the beach, I was in New York with my family as we gathered around my grandmother in the hospital. It was hard for me because she was my only living grandparent and for so long, I had been mad with her. I had always wanted a grandmother who spoiled her grandchildren and was ever so sweet, but my grandmother did not fit that stereotype. I was mad because the one grandparents' day that she was present for at my school, she spent most of her time with Leah. I had been holding that against her all that time. All I could do was pray to God that I got a chance to say how sorry I was and that I loved her.

I got the chance to see her and say my apologies and just hold her hand, letting her know how much I loved her. She looked so frail and weak. I was left in the room by myself with her because Dad fainted after seeing his mother. By the time I got back downstairs, I was all cried out. Dad seemed to be okay and honestly, it was the only time I could remember seeing the emotional and weak side of my dad. Watching his mother dying was not easy, and at one point, he went off to the bathroom for some space. After a while, he did not come out. After his previous fainting spell, it had Jack and CJ running into the bathroom to make sure he was okay. I will always wonder what went on in that bathroom because they stayed in there for a while. They came out a few minutes later and thankfully Dad was okay.

At the end of the week, we left New York and I was back to school. It was only about a week later when I received an early morning phone call from Mom telling me that grandma had passed away. When I got the news, a tear rolled down my check and I lay back down. I knew that I was heading back to New York and this time, it was for a funeral.

I was taking some great courses that semester. One in particular was our general psychology class. I was a pre-med student, but for some reason that course spoke to me. I found myself wondering if I was in the right major. It was not that I thought I could not do the academic part of it, but I found myself wondering if I would have to give up so many of my dreams, like a husband and a family, just so I could achieve one dream— being a doctor. I started to think and pray, and one day, I called my family to inform them that I was switching my major to psychology—child and adolescent development to be exact. I would still be working with kids, but this way, I could achieve all the things that were important to me. I had made the right decision, or at least at the time, that was what I thought.

Winter had given way to spring, and that meant more students were out on the lawn enjoying the weather. Okay, so technically that could mean a high of fifty degrees and people were out in flip-flops and shorts, but we were excited; enough of the snow. At one point in late January to early February, we had experienced snow every Thursday for about three or four weeks straight. Monday would come around, and the snow would start to melt, only to have it start again that Thursday. Beth's boyfriend had actually gotten stuck in Lynchburg after coming down from Boston to see her Valentine's weekend. He did not get to leave until that following Tuesday. Needless to say, the sun and warm weather had become a commodity that we appreciated.

Tom and a few of the guys from his dorm were out in the intramural field throwing around a baseball. I figured it was the perfect opportunity to pull out CJ's old glove and join them. I went back to the dorm and threw on my *Umbro* shorts, grabbed my glove, and joined the boys. I got situated and one of the guys threw me a fly ball. I backed up to line up perfectly with the ball and catch it in my glove. The glove was up, and I was patiently waiting for the ball to come down into my glove. Oh, the ball came down all right; it came down right on my face—my nose to be exact. All I heard was a crack, and there was blood gushing from my nose. Everyone came running over and Tom, of course, had plenty of jokes at the ready like why I had to catch the ball with my face. I just looked at him and he was off to get me some napkins and ice. I was eventually laughing, and I knew this meant a field trip to the ER. So much for our night plans of seeing the second *Lord of the Rings* in our dollar theater.

We piled into Tom's car and headed off for the hospital, where we spent the next six hours. Fortunately, I was not in a considerable amount of pain. After being there so long, the doctor finally came in, only to tell me that my nose was too swollen for them to officially say if it was broken. They said that it probably was and that I should expect to see a black eye in the next day or so and to take plenty of pain medication. The only upside was that I got this eye mask that held ice. We left, and all I could think was *Why didn't I leave well enough alone?* The next day, sure enough, I woke up with a black eye. I was thankful that it was the weekend and there was a fresh blanket of snow on the ground. I could hide out for a while. By Monday, I was able to cover up my black eye with some makeup and not look too much like a raccoon. My friends now had something on me they would not soon let me live down.

With spring in full swing and the semester drawing to a close, we found ourselves spending all our free time together. One day it was a picnic on campus and another it was a nice steak dinner. One Saturday in particular, the guys decided they wanted to take Beth, Alex, and me to see a waterfall they had heard some of the other guys in their dorm talking about. Alex was not much of the exercising type, not that she needed to be, as she probably weighed 110 pounds soaking wet, so the thought of walking a great distance did not appeal to her much. Beth was excited to just get out for some fresh air and exercise. I figured with us being situated in the mountains, this was a sight to see. We got ready in our hiking gear— shorts, a T-shirt, and tennis shoes—and set out to meet the guys and be on our way.

When we arrived at the park, we soon discovered that the guys didn't know exactly where the waterfall was, so this would be as much a search as it was a hike. We girls figured as long as it was not too far away, we were game. We walked, enjoying the scenery along the way and stopping to take pictures when the area seemed right. At one particular spot, we stopped to look off the bluff that they had turned into a stopping area along the path. Off the far right, we saw a little trickle of water coming from the mountain. It was quaint, but we were just hoping that this was not the waterfall that the guys brought us up the mountain to see. We kept walking and walking and walking. Before we knew it, we were a mile or so away from the bluff and at the end of the trail.

Looking at the river following next to us, Beth, Alex, and I realized that the trickle was indeed the waterfall, and we had all been duped; some waterfall. We turned around and started to head back in the direction we came. It was at this same moment that the sky opened up on us a torrential rain storm. With lightning and thunder all around us, we ran the two miles or so back down the mountain and to our cars. By now, Beth, Alex, and I were fuming, tired, and because of the storm, soaking wet. The ride back to the dorms was a quiet one and when the guys dropped us off at our dorm, we simply told them we would see them the next morning. We were too tired, wet, and hungry to bother with the possibility of seeing them at any point later that night. We vowed then and there to check out any future places the guys wanted to take us—we did not want this happening again.

My friendship with Tom had developed so that I found myself having feelings for him. While he admitted to not feeling the same, he did not rule out the possibility; there was hope. At the end of the semester, we found ourselves enjoying slushies and talking about us. We just didn't know what was happening or where anything was going. The summer was before us, and we knew that anything was possible. I hated the end of the year because I knew that meant I had to say good-bye to people I had come to love. Some were graduating, and some were transferring to other schools. Alex, in particular, was transferring to a school closer to home that had her major, and I did not know when I would see her next. We promised to stay in touch because our friendship was too important to us. I left knowing that I had grown so much as a person, both emotionally and spiritually. I was so excited to get through the summer and get back for the next school year.

# CHAPTER SEVEN

*Some people come into our lives and quickly go. Some stay for a while and leave footprints on our hearts. And we are never, ever the same.*

*—Source Unknown*

S ummer had begun, and I was supposed to start working for my old boss again. Unfortunately, things did not work out, and I was frantically looking for a summer job. I remembered one of my RAs telling some of us about a camp she would be working at in Virginia as a counselor. I figured it was worth a shot because I had nothing better to do. Again, I struck out; they already hired all the female counselors they needed for the summer. I was now close to my wit's end. I had no clue where to start looking for a job at home. Some may say that fate or destiny stepped in, but I knew it was completely God. I received a letter in the mail informing me that one of the female counselors could not make it and if I wanted, the job was mine. I was excited because I had a job, but at the same time, I was scared. In a year's time, I found myself going into another new situation where I only knew one or two people. Rational thought took over: I needed the money, so I took the job. My family and I set out for Camp Happyland (yes, that really was the name). CJ had always joked about places in Florida being behind God's back because they were just so far out there. As my family made the last hour trek in the trip, that was exactly how we felt.

We finally arrived, and I asked them if it was too late to change my mind. I was among the last to arrive, and instantly I felt like an outsider. Mercifully, the camp director, Captain Charles and his wife, Grace, were so kind and made me feel right at home. My family could not stay long as they were heading back home, so they got something to eat and soon they were gone, leaving me all alone. Orientation was beginning that night, so it was off to the chapel to get to know one another; boy did we. We played get-to-know-you games and laughed. That first week was tiring, and I found myself wondering if being at camp for two months was worth it. I missed my family and the comfort of home, and trying to adjust to a new environment was proving to be harder than I thought; adjusting to college life was easier. I knew deep down inside that it was the fear of the unknown that was trying to get me to quit and just go home. I had to keep reminding myself that I was not a quitter and that I would not let fear rob me of what could turn out to be something great.

The second day of being there, I received a call from Tom, and knowing that I could look forward to calls from him on the weekends helped to ease my anxiety. I was also meeting some great people from all over the world. I met Daisy and Danielle, twin sisters from Canada; Eli and Quinn, both from England; and Cole, Tara, and Eva. At first glance, it was difficult to distinguish between Daisy and Danielle. They were both blondes of average height. It did not take long, however, to learn the difference could be found in their personalities. Where Danielle was older and outgoing, Daisy was quiet and kept to herself. I found myself gravitating more toward Daisy because I saw a lot of myself in her and that was a comfort. Eli and Quinn were English—need I say more? Eli was slender and stood at five foot ten or so, where Quinn was more muscular and stood at six foot even. Cole was about Quinn's height and had a build like Eli, but with dark hair. Cole and Quinn quickly became partners in crime. I will just say I let them hold my camera once and I found pictures of Cole performing a balancing act on the fence and a picture of him showing off his legs. Tara had short blonde hair, an angelic face, and a heart the size of Texas. Eva became my partner in crime, with the two of us forming a bond almost instantly. It was not like these people were going to eat me alive, right? Right?

I made it through orientation unscathed, and I was looking at facing the first full week of camp. It was a girls' camp, so the guys, in theory, had the week off until the following week, which was the boy's camp. Mind you, a week at camp did not mean Sunday to Saturday. A week at camp most of the times were Monday to Saturday, but there were times it was a Tuesday to Thursday, depending on what type of camp it was that particular week. This also meant that "Sunday" fell on a Friday or Thursday. See how easy it was to get your days mixed up?

For some strange reason, this all-girls week pushed the camp to capacity, and girls were being pulled in from everywhere to cover a cabin. I drew the privilege of sharing a cabin with the camp director's oldest daughter, Chelsea. She was a five foot two, dark-haired beauty who pulled off the tomboy look with such grace that you secretly wanted to handicap her just so you could get the advantage, even if for a second. Of course I would not because she was as nice as could be. I felt especially bad for her when she discovered she would have some of the youngest girls on campus while I had girls who averaged age nine or ten. I did have one girl, Marie, who was six, but she was in my cabin with the other Asian girls who were at camp. The beginning of the week, for me, was cake.

The other girls in my cabin were from random corps and they were all getting along wonderfully well. The problems started with a girl from Chelsea's cabin who had grown so attached to her that she did not want to leave her side. When it came time for the girls to go to their year groups, we learned the first day that we had to distract this girl or I would have to take her kicking and screaming from Chelsea's side—that just was not good for my health. Anytime we saw Chelsea, we would distract this little girl in conversation or divert her attention elsewhere until it was time for her to go back with Chelsea. The week progressed and my only respite was the hour break when the girls were at the pool or at night when I had put them to bed.

Nighttime provided an hour or so chance for the staff to have adult conversation and just sympathize with each other. On the nights I went out, if I was lucky, I got a chance to talk briefly on the phone with Tom. He was also spending his summer at a camp as a counselor. Since Chelsea's boyfriend, Ben, was at camp, I volunteered most nights to stay in the cabin with the girls. He was one of the lifeguards at camp, and he looked as though he just stepped from the pages of a catalogue or just off the set of a model shoot. To me, Chelsea and Ben were that fairytale couple you heard about but just did not believe in because it sounded too good to be true. Yet, here they were in real life. I will never forget my first real interaction with Ben. Chelsea could not make it down to the pool one afternoon so she sent me with a message for him—"143." I, of course, asked what in the world that was supposed to mean. "I love you" was her reply. I just had to ask. I made my way to the pool with the girls and searched for Ben to deliver the message. I could not resist sounding disgusted to have to give such a message (Who am I kidding? I kind of was.), and our brother/sister relationship was born.

The week progressed nicely—that was until the talent show. As I said before, my cabin was split in groups—half were Asian and the other half a mix of girls from different places that found similarity in each other, as they were not Asian. The Asian half had already prepared a performance with their mothers and corps leaders, and the other half of my cabin decided to put together a dance, minus a girl or two. The night of the talent show arrived and each group got up and performed their hearts out. When all was said and done, I was proudly cheering because my girls won—the Asian group, that is. That left the other half of my cabin rather upset and in tears. Later in the night, as they were getting ready for bed, I realized that one of the girls was crying. I came to find out that the "losing" side of the cabin was tormenting the "winning" side; the mean and hurtful things that little girls can say. After I made sure that the offended girl was okay and reprimanded the tormentors, I told everyone that it was time to go to bed. I was tired and officially spent from what occurred in the past hour or so. I informed the girls that I did not want to hear a peep from them. I went to bed and asked God to give me the wisdom to handle the situation.

The next day was camp Sunday, so that meant we had our church service. It also meant we got to sleep later, and with the way things went the night before, I needed it. Unfortunately, that morning picked up right where the night left off and my "angels" were no longer talking to each other. Divided by race and a ribbon, I was more determined to bring reconciliation to my cabin. The question was—how? Breakfast came and went and no change. We had our parade and were in the chapel, lining up to go to the bathroom before the service began. It was as they were coming out from the bathroom and lining up to go in that I got my idea. I decided that if they were not going to talk to each other, they were not going to talk period. I lined them up one girl from the winning side and one girl from the losing side, alternating until I was out of girls. I told them that if they wanted to talk to anyone, they had to talk to the person sitting next to them and they could not talk over each other to avoid it. One of the girls actually looked at me and said, "I know what you are trying to do. You are trying to make us talk to each other again—it won't work." Not that it would have taken a genius to figure out my plan, but still she had me. I simply replied that it was indeed my intention and that we would see who was right.

The service was beautiful, and I dare say that by lunchtime, that same girl came back to me saying that they were all friends again. With that, she was off, with her arm around the shoulder of a girl from the winning side. Seeing that they had settled things on their own (with a little help from me), I was proud of my girls. I could not help but think that if I made it through this week—what many called the worst week of camp—I would be okay the rest of the summer.

After that week, the summer began to roll by. I eventually got into the routine of things and felt I had found another home away from home. Tom and I were talking when we could get the chance and when we could actually catch each other on the phone. Things were perfect—until I checked my phone during a break I had late one afternoon and I happily realized that I had a message from Chloe. It had been a while since high school, but we still kept in touch. The message she left for me rocked my world to the core forever. I called her, and she told me she had been assaulted. That was just the first blow. She proceeded to tell me that she was pregnant and getting married. The two incidents were not related. The father of the baby and husband-to-be was the same guy she had told me about only a few months prior. By the time I hung up the phone, too many emotions were going through me at once. I instantly felt anger and rage and yet at the same time, I was hurting for my friend. When I told the head female counselor, Phoebe, who was also my RA at Liberty, of the news that I just received, she told me to take some time away from the kids to recuperate fully. I thankfully took the opportunity and before I left, I could tell that Quinn was concerned, but I just could not deal with him at the moment. It did not help that I had not heard from Tom in a while. I got back to my cabin and just cried. I was aching for my friend, knowing that I could do nothing for her because she was miles away. I was feeling her pain as if it was my own. I just needed a shoulder to cry—someone to tell me that it would be okay and bring back the innocence that I once knew.

Tom and I eventually decided to give a relationship a try. It was that same night that Eva had to go and bring up the fact that Quinn seemed to have an interest in me. All of a sudden, I went from no guys to two guys in one evening. I shrugged it off as best as I could because I knew I could not deal with it at the moment. I finally had the guy that I wanted for months. Why would I want someone who was funny, charming, intelligent, good looking, and British? Who was I kidding?—I was a mess. While Tom was what I had wanted for a while now,

Quinn was all I had dreamed about. Caught between the affections of two guys who both had what I was looking for, I needed something else to distract me.

After getting over the initial shock of Chloe's news, I put my all into work. The following week, I came down with bronchitis, and I was out for a few days. I had not heard from Tom, and Quinn was quickly becoming the center of my attention. It did not feel as if I was in a relationship with anyone, and I was starting to wonder why he had even asked in the first place. In the time I was sick, I was comforted to know that Quinn was praying for me and he even made me a get well gift during craft time with his guys. By the end of that week, I finally heard from Tom. He thought that we were better off as friends and he was not ready for a commitment. I did not know what happened during the time we did not talk, but I was relieved. I no longer had to feel guilty for talking to Quinn, much less the growing attraction I felt toward him. I was now free to explore what could possibly be between us.

Summer was quickly coming to an end, with only about two weeks of camp remaining. It was one of our weekends off, but the whole camp was headed to King's Dominion. Not that I did not enjoy amusement parks, but I've said it before: I am not all that big on rides. The thing I was looking forward to was a day with Quinn. The ride to the park was filled with talking and laughter, and by the time we arrived, we had split ourselves into groups with which we would explore the park. Some rides I enjoyed, especially if Quinn was sitting next to me;

some of them I gave one look and said, "You must be out of your mind." On those rides, I happily waited nearby for those who chose to risk life and limb. Sometimes, I would have someone waiting with me and other times, it was nice to have a moment by myself to just think and remember to enjoy every minute of this day. By the time we left the park, we were one exhausted group of young adults. More than likely we would sleep the whole way back to camp. Well, at least I did. Conveniently for me, Quinn was sitting next to me, so I had a nice shoulder to sleep on until we got back to camp. It was not until later when Eva and I were alone that she informed me of the look in Quinn's eyes as I slept soundly on his shoulder. She described it as a look of adoration. Now what girl would not want that? I know it was something I had always dreamed about, considering that I had been known to snore and drool a little. The only thing that would have made that day any better would have been actually getting to see that look of adoration on his face.

I t was one of those weeks at camp. It was the next to last week, and everyone was tired, exhausted, and pushing to give their all to the end. We were desperately trying to get as much sleep as possible, starting to pack a little, and frankly, our nerves were on edge. But we learned in orientation that it was important that each week and camp get our best, so we were getting through this—one way or another. It was at this time that the staff really started to pull together and lean on each other.

No matter what differences we had, at this point, it was practically null and void. If you saw someone dragging, you tried to pick them up and in effect, pick yourself up. Quinn and I were able to do that for each other that week. We both were having a rough time with our cabins—I think him more so than I. One day we crossed paths on the canteen deck, one of us having just dropped our kids off at the pool and the other taking our kids back to the cabin to change. For a moment, we stopped and just hugged each other, knowing what the other felt. In that hug, I felt safe and protected. I found strength to continue on, and knowing that I would soon have to let go, I did not want to. Eventually, we went our separate ways for the day. Even now, I think back to that hug and what it meant to me.

One week to go and as happy as I was to be getting ready to go home, I was also sad because of all the friends I had to say good-bye to. Chelsea and her family, Ben, Eva, Cole, Tara—and those were just the ones that lived in the States. Daisy and Danielle promised to come back the following year, so I could not wait till then to see them. The saddest good-bye of all would be Quinn. I didn't want to say good-bye. The week went by, and before I knew it, it was the last day we had kids for the summer. A band from England came in and was going to be giving a concert for us in the chapel. Quinn and I discussed the possibility of sitting together for the occasion if it was at all possible. I will never forget when he walked into the chapel. Our eyes met, and for a few moments in time, it was as if we were the only two people in the room. Given my prior cynicism on love and the like, to experience that was quite remarkable. I had always heard that said, but to hear it and experience it are quite different. We spoke shortly, and he went off to sit with his guys. As I turned, I got the feeling someone was watching me. To my surprise and somewhat amusement, the caretaker's wife and the camp secretary had both seen Quinn and me. They grinned like Cheshire cats at me. I at least took joy in knowing that I was not imagining things and that I really had experienced that moment.

The time ticked by and we found ourselves having our last meal together. Unfortunately, I did not get to have it with Quinn. By the time I reached the restaurant, the tables had filled up quickly and Chelsea, Ben, and I had to sit in the outer area, away from everyone else. While I was saddened by this fact, it gave me time to get to know Chelsea and Ben better. We joked, laughed, and all in all, had a good time. I knew I had found really good friends in those two. I only hoped I would get to see them again. The meal came to an end and people were taking pictures and some were saying their final good-byes. Some were leaving for home from the restaurant, and others were heading back to camp for a final night. As Captain Charles had told us a couple of weeks prior, we would not likely meet as we were as a group on this side of heaven. We had come together for a short time and were heading off in many different directions to continue on in our paths.

Back at camp, I was hanging around Quinn and Cole, as Quinn would be spending some time with Cole and his family. He was not heading back to England just yet, and some of our friends had generously offered him to stay with them until his return. He pulled me off to the side, and we started to say our good-bye. I did not want to, and I was hoping it was more of a "see you later." We did not want to think of how things would or could work out between us. It nearly broke my heart when he asked, "Why do you have to live in America?" Reluctantly, I gave him a hug, knowing I did not want to let go as I did not know when I would get to do it again—if I got to do it again. In the span of one summer, I was able to meet a great Christian guy who appreciated me for who I was, and I was able to appreciate him for who he was. I knew I would just have to leave it in God's hands. Slowly, I turned back to head to the office and wait for my family to show up. Shoulders hunched, I walked in with tears in my eyes, knowing I just said good-bye to the first guy to look me in the eyes and tell me I was beautiful, knowing that he truly meant it.

Summer only lasted a few more weeks for me when I got home. I was able to perform my maid-of-honor duties at Chloe's bridal shower. Soon I was on my way back to school for leadership training. Quinn was still in the country making his way back to DC to fly back to England. I had one last chance to see him before he left. This time, he was at Eva's house with her family, and she informed me they would be close by. Oh, how I wanted to get in a car and drive to hug Quinn one last time. Sadly, I had a wedding to be in and that took precedence. I knew I would hear from Quinn as soon as he got home, and that would have to suffice. Chloe's wedding proved to be a beautiful one, despite the many holdups of the day. For starters, two of us were missing our bridesmaid dresses. The seamstress had promised they would be ready in time for the wedding. Five minutes before the wedding and there were still no dresses. Another ten minutes went by and not a word. Finally, Chloe's uncle went over to the store (which was not a short distance from the church) and retrieved our dresses. With our dresses finally in hand and the other bridesmaids helping us get dressed, the wedding was finally underway—even if it was forty-five minutes after it was supposed to start. With those issues out of the way, the rest of the day ran smoothly. When all was said and done, we sent Chloe and her new husband, Chase, on their way. I knew that the next day I would be on my way back to school and thinking of how close Quinn had been and yet so far away.

# CHAPTER EIGHT

*Character cannot be developed in ease and quiet. Only through experience of trial and suffering can the soul be strengthened, ambition inspired, and success achieved.*
—*Helen Keller*

The first semester of my sophomore year progressed as well as I could have expected. I was a little sad because many of the friends I hung out with the previous year were either at another school or on a different hall. I had to adjust to the change, but I was fighting it. Both my roommates were freshman and busy taking advantage of college life. Slowly I made friends with the girls in the two rooms next to mine, partly because a few of them were on the leadership team with me and partly because we seemed to get along and they were close by. In the room right next to me, 205, lived Emma, Samantha, and Sophie. All three had naturally curly hair, varying in shades of color. Emma had blondish brown hair and a quick wit. She was a transfer student and, unfortunately, also a Carolina fan; I tried not to hold that against her. Samantha had brown hair, and we clicked really well. She was on the hall with me the previous year and had been my prayer leader the second semester. Lastly, Sophie was the redhead of the group. I did not get to see much of her. She was an honor student who always had a project or work to finish. Both Emma and Sam were on leadership with me. In room 203 lived Daphne, Lani, and Lily. This room was always filled with laughter. Daphne was in the marching band and had a sense of humor that always made me smile. I came to discover that when I broke my nose that spring, Daphne had been in the field with a friend and seen the whole thing. When I told the story of that day, she looked at me and said, "You were that girl?!" Talk about your connections and six degrees of separation. Lani, who was also on leadership, became someone I could lean on and trust. Put her and Daphne together and the laughs would just continue to roll. Lastly, there was Lily who was also had naturally curly reddish hair. She too was busy and normally would be heading out the door when I stopped to visit. Eventually, I was spending more time in their rooms than in my own room.

One Friday afternoon that September, I was waiting for Luke to get out of classes so we could go home for the weekend. Dad knew I was coming in, and I was hoping to surprise Mom. It was close to noon, so I had at least three hours to burn. I was already dressed for travel—a T-shirt, my *Umbro* shorts, and flip-flops. I found myself in 203 hanging out with Daphne and Lani. We were just talking and having a good time laughing at the jokes and stories we were telling each other. Someone said something so funny I found myself doubled over in laughter. I guess I should have mentioned that the doorways in our rooms were made of wood paneling. As I was bent over in laughter, I found myself popping up rather quickly from the slight prick I felt a second earlier in my backside. When I ran my hand over the area, I discovered I had picked up a splinter. This of course got us all laughing even harder. Only I would break my nose and get a splinter in my rear end in the same year. Now I found myself with a splinter in a very unusual place, and Daphne was again present to witness the incident. Thinking it was just a simple splinter, I attempted to pull it out. I soon found it was larger and longer than I had originally thought, and that meant I would need some help.

I found myself in Megan's room, Tom's sister and one of my RAs, as she attempted to remove it for me; that is friendship right there. By now the piece of wood had split into two, proving to be rather difficult to remove. Luckily, one of the nursing students on the hall was in her room, and we asked if she could assist us. I knew I wanted to bond with the girls on the hall more, but that was not what I had in mind. Try as she might, she couldn't get it out either. By now, it had become rather clear that I needed to go see a doctor. Megan made a call to the on-campus doctor's office. After the explanation of the situation, I could hear the laughter on the other end of the phone even as they suggested I go to the emergency room. After my visit there earlier that year, I knew it would take too long and I needed help as soon as possible so I could be ready to meet Luke to go home. I decided to head to a doctor's office off campus that I had previously visited. The nursing student who tried in vain to remove my splinter volunteered to take me. Now I found myself in her car, with one side of my rear end kind of up in the air and resting on a pillow. To say it hurt would have been an understatement.

When we arrived at the doctor's office, filling out the necessary paperwork proved to be interesting. When I got to the line *Reason for visit*, I started to wonder what I should put. I realized I had to be honest, no matter how crazy it sounded. When it came time for me to go back to see the doctor, I received more than a few chuckles from the nurses. I had already learned that in situations like this, I had two choices: laugh or cry. I most often chose to laugh, and this occasion was no different. By the time I saw the doctor, he too was having a hard time controlling the chuckles. It was a funny situation, so how could I be offended? I was making jokes to keep the mood light. After examining the situation, the doctor informed me that there was only one way to get the splinter out safely: he was going to have to cut it out. All I could think was: "Are you kidding me? All this for a stupid splinter in the side of my rear?!"

The main reason he had to cut it out was that it was split in two and pulling it out might leave smaller pieces of wood. He did not want to risk that, as it was treated wood. Before he cut me open, he had to numb the area. He warned me that it might hurt a little bit. Yeah, what he forgot to tell me was that it would hurt *a lot*. So much so that I was to the point I would have just rather left the thing in. Since I was holding the nurse's arm as he gave me the shot, I am pretty sure she was more relieved than I was when he was done. I am also pretty sure that her hearing went back to normal as well. As much as I wished I could have seen what he was doing, I was relieved when he was done. Two pieces of wood and six stitches later, I was on my way.

The ride home with Luke was interesting to say the least. I received many jokes, especially from my family, about the whole ordeal. Thankfully I was still numb for most of the ride home, so pain was not that much of an issue. I was just looking forward to spending time with my family. Unfortunately, Mom decided to make a quick visit to Bradley and his family in Georgia the night I got home, so I was all alone. The day just could not get any worse. Yeah, right. By the time I was ready for bed, all the pain medication had worn off and sleeping proved to be rather hard. I spent that night on the couch sleeping on my stomach. I would also spend that Saturday in the same spot and position. Try as my dad might, he could not get my mom to leave any sooner. They did not get home until much later that night, and as surprised as she was to see me, I was already disappointed. I would be leaving that next day, and my stitches had already proved to be pain in the butt—literally and figuratively.

A week later, I was thankful to have my stitches gone. That semester proved to be the toughest I had seen yet. Academically, I was pretty stable, and I had no real concerns there. Socially, however, I was feeling the pinch. Things between Tom and I had become strained at best. I found that I was actually trying to avoid him because it seemed as if I didn't exist to him. I had friends on and off the dorm, but I was expecting things to be as they had been the year before. As excited as I was at the beginning of the semester to be a part of hall leadership, it was starting to prove to be a little more than I could handle. The only comfort I had was that others felt the same way I did. At one point, there was a concert happening on campus, and a few of us from leadership went. Needless to say, it ran long, but we did not want to leave because we all could feel the presence of God in that place and that is where we wanted to be. We knew we were missing an important hall meeting and that the consequences could be grave, but in that moment, being so close to God was more important.

When we got back, we were given those stern looks and a long talking to, but it was worth it. I am not one to quit, so I decided to tough it out. The situation with Quinn did not make things any easier. While we finally admitted to having feelings for each other, there was the issue of the ocean that separated us, my dislike of flying, and, as he put it, "the controlled atmosphere of camp." We would talk for hours on end, coming to an impasse on the whole issue. I found myself looking for perspectives from friends. I found myself going to Ryan and asking his opinion. He gave me the best advice—to let go and let God. I was trying too hard to make things work. If they were going to happen, there was nothing I could or could not do to help that matter.

The semester wore on, and things just continued to wear on me. By mid-October, I was so sick my family had to come take me home. At home, I went to see my regular physician and learned that part of my sickness was due to exhaustion. Could I honestly say I was surprised? I had assumed I could do all like I had before and that I would not feel the effects. More importantly, I thought I could do it all on my own. By the end of the week, I was headed back to LU. This time, I hoped I learned my lesson. I finished the semester as strong as possible with hopes that the next semester would be better.

I was home for the holidays and loving every minute of it. Christmas morning arrived, and I was not exactly expecting anything much. By then, I learned it was not about the getting but rather what you could give and the time you shared with those you love. My mom handed me this box about the size of a large music box. I opened it to discover another box inside. I did this about two or three more times to discover a small and final box. Inside, I found a key, and my mom directed me to the windows. Outside, there was a car with a big red bow on top just for me. No, it was not brand new, but it meant the world to me that my parents sacrificed so I could have a car for school. My only problem was driving the five hours to school by myself. I was scared half out of my mind. I finally decided to just drive up with Luke and when I felt comfortable driving the distance by myself, I would.

With a new semester before me, I chose to do something I had not done before (and something I would not do again)—I took eighteen credit hours. Any student knows that fifteen hours is considered a full load, with twelve hours being the minimum to be considered a full-time student. Eighteen was definitely pushing it. I reasoned in my mind that three of those classes were only meeting once a week so I would be okay. For the most part, I was. I was able to balance classes and my leadership responsibilities well enough, but social activities were limited. This time, I only had one of the freshman roommates from the semester before. Bridget, Luke's girlfriend, had moved in with us, and both of them had a full load juggling classes and boyfriends. I found myself always reading something for a class, in particular English. We always had a quiz, which meant I always had to be prepared. Only one of my psychology classes was not much of a concern, so I felt pretty good.

It had come to that time of year where my sinuses were bothering me, and on most days, that was not a problem. Unfortunately, this day was a Thursday, which was my busiest day of the week. I had classes that started at 10:50 that morning, and I would not be done until six o'clock that evening. I took a Tylenol Sinus to get me through classes. By the time I got back to my dorm that afternoon, I was feeling all right, but my day was far from over. Thursday also meant hall meeting, prayer groups, and then our resident hall leadership meeting, or RHLM for short. I still had some pressure around my eyes and forehead, so I took a DayQuil to get me through the rest of the day. I figured it was a good six hours since I had the Tylenol so I was good.

Emma came over to ask me if I wanted to make a Wal-Mart run with her, and I felt up to it, so we were off. We were not there long, and Emma was noticing that my speech was sounding kind of funny. I just assumed I was tired from the long day I went through. By the time we got back to the dorm, I could hear the slur of my speech quite clearly. Emma suggested I just lie down for a while, and frankly, it sounded like a good idea. I don't know how long I was resting my eyes before I got an instant message from my SLD, Kelly. We were supposed to have our meeting at seven o'clock, so she wanted to know if I was ready to come down. I walked down the hall to her room a few minutes later, even more tired than when I lay down a few minutes before. I was not in her room five minutes when Kelly asked if I was okay. I just said I was not feeling all that well. Not too long after that, she noticed that my face looked a little puffy and I was starting to sway. This entire time, I had been sitting on her bed, but now I knew something was wrong. The room was spinning, and I sounded as if I was drunk.

Kelly immediately called campus emergency, and within a few minutes, they were in the room checking my vitals. My pulse rate was up some, but they said that was to be expected since I took some DayQuil. With my speech problems, the dizziness, and swelling of my face, they advised that I go to the ER.

Not wanting to wait or pay for the ambulance, I opted to have someone drive me. Most of the leadership team that was currently on the hall was aware of the situation and generally concerned. It was close to the time for hall meeting, so as Megan was taking me down the stairs to her waiting car, we ran into girls coming up the stairs, including Bridget. She heard me say something to her and assumed I was drunk. By the time Megan pulled up in front of the ER doors, I was too disoriented to even walk. Before I left the car to take a seat in the awaiting wheelchair, I looked to heaven to lift up a prayer for God to spare me. I was truly scared because I had no idea what was going on or how it would play out. Even though I knew the doctors would do their best to help me, I knew God had the final say.

Thankfully, I did not have to wait as long as I did the last time to see the doctor. They assessed me and asked the necessary questions, but I was just feeling really woozy. I figured it was about time to call my parents and let them know what was going on. I got a hold of my dad, but he could not understand what I was saying, so I handed the phone to Megan and let her do the talking. By now, the doctors had given me something to help with the tongue swelling aspect of things and were also checking my balance. When I sat back down, I asked Megan how I did. Apparently, when I thought I was standing up straight, I was leaning to one side. By the time they were done doing their evaluation, they could only conclude that the drugs may have interacted with each other; I was thinking maybe an allergic reaction. Either way, I vowed then to stay away from DayQuil or NyQuil. I called Dad back to let him know I was on my way back to campus. By the time I got back, I was so exhausted that I just collapsed into bed. Tomorrow would be a better day.

Thankfully I did not have class on Friday, so I slept in. I woke that morning to discover that I had a lisp and things were pretty foggy in my head. I took the medication the doctor gave me only to have a tremble reaction to it. I had to call the pharmacy to have something else called in for me. I got a call from my mom to find out that Dad had not told her anything that happened the night before until that morning. He reasoned that if he had, she would have wanted to drive up to me, as they were already in Spartanburg. As twisted as his reasoning sounded, I did understand why he did what he did. I struggled to have a conversation with my mom as things were still foggy, and it proved to be difficult to get complete thoughts together. I was afraid to be stuck like that for the rest of my life, and then what would I have going for me? As far I knew, my intelligence was what made me who I was and set me apart from others. I had already informed Quinn of what happened, and he was checking up to make sure I was okay when he could. My friends thought it was cute to hear me talk with a lisp. All I could think was how frustrating it was, and I was just praying to wake up from this nightmare. To make things worse, Chelsea and her family were in town that weekend and we were meeting up for dinner. As excited as I was to see them all again, I knew that my lisp would be a problem. We got to the restaurant and unfortunately I wanted to order my favorite dish—Chipotle Chicken—but that proved too much of a challenge to say. Finally, I just pointed to the picture in the menu to inform the waitress of what I wanted. I enjoyed my time with them and was sad to see them go.

The week progressed, and I did as little talking in class as I could. While the fog had thankfully lifted, I still had my little friend with me. Each night, I found myself going to bed praying that when I woke the next morning, it would be gone. By Thursday, I had come to grips with the possible fact that I would have that lisp for the rest of my life. I could have cried. I just wanted things to go back to normal. I went to bed that night and awoke Friday morning to discover the lisp gone. If I had ever taken my intelligence for granted before, I learned from that experience to appreciate the gifts God gives us. You just never know when they might disappear.

Things with Tom had definitely taken a turn for the better, and I was glad to have my friend back. It did not take long before things became interesting, to say the least. We were spending more time together, studying late at night in the computer lab, going to late nights, and just being who we had always been. One night he said he picked on me because he liked me. I thought maybe I was hearing wrong. He then went on to repeat himself. All I could think was I just had three months until the end of the semester and now this bomb. I just had to assume he meant it in some other way than I was thinking and that I was overreacting. I did not need any more confusion in my life. I was trying to figure out how to work out studying abroad, with the possibility of being closer to Quinn, finishing out what proved to be a tough academic semester, and just staying afloat. I went to bed that night having my instant messenger away message stating: "You know, when they yell 'Duck' it's always too late." Ryan came to my rescue again by informing me to not want *a* guy, want *the* guy and not to waste my time with the other ones.

Spring break came and went, and when it was time to go back to school, I decided that I was ready to drive my car back to campus. I was scared, of course, but my parents prayed with me before I left and I said a prayer as I pulled out of the driveway to begin my five-hour trek. When I arrived at school, I was proud of myself. I had overcome a fear and I knew that I could do more if I just put my mind to it. The remainder of the semester was far better than the beginning. I finally learned to balance class, leadership responsibilities, and a social life. With both my roommates spending most of their free time with their boyfriends, I had become the "fourth roommate" of Emma, Samantha, and Sophie. There were times I would pull my mattress into their room for sleepovers. Of course, that really just led to tickle fights and "jumping on the mattress" wars.

I soon found myself attending church with Samantha and even going on their youth retreat. Previously, I was just going to campus church. I decided I needed to branch out in my understanding of different denominations. Samantha was involved with a local Church of God. Needless to say, the youth retreat was unlike any I had gone to before. With the camps I had gone to during high school, you knew that most kids (including myself) did not want to be there and were only there to make their parents happy or because they had to be. For the first time in my life, I saw youth groups that actually wanted to be where they were. They actually could not wait to get to the services. I spent most of my high school life waiting for the services to be over. They could not wait to see what God had for them. How was this possible? They were teenagers, and the teenagers I knew and had been in high school with could have cared less. What was so different here? I quickly found my answer. Their youth leaders and the adults around them did not simply tell them how they should live—they led by example. They knew that their youth leaders were not perfect and never tried to be. They were simply real with them, and I saw firsthand what I had missed out on. I saw how the youth leaders really cared for their youth group. That weekend proved to be an eye-opening experience for me in so many ways. My high school years were so focused on religion, and I knew I needed to focus on my relationship. I knew God had so much more to teach me about a relationship with Him.

I took a few more trips that semester as well, including one back home with Tom and Megan and my first trip to Kentucky. As the semester grew to a close, I was planning on making another trip—to England. I had been accepted into a study abroad program, and I was excited at the great opportunity that lay ahead of me. Not to mention it would be an opportunity to be closer to Quinn. We still kept up our communication as best as we could, and I was looking forward to seeing him that summer.

Tom and I were thick as thieves, and it bothered me that I was closer to him than I was to Quinn. It bothered me how close we were and how comfortable I was with him. Tom knew me so much better than Quinn, and he knew how to make me laugh. All I could think was that we tried before and it did not work. That was it. Case closed. One of the last days of the semester, Tom told me that he did not think that Quinn was all that great and frankly he did not deserve me. It bothered me and stuck with me all at the same time. Before leaving, we talked and tried to clear the air about many things. We came to the conclusion that the "us" back then was bad timing— the wrong timing, making it the wrong thing. I left that semester thinking I was not coming back as I would be in England that fall. Many of my confusions would finally be laid to rest.

By the time summer had begun, I had gotten word from Quinn that he was having problems getting his visa and was not sure if he would make it back. I kept praying all would work out, but by the time I was ready to head off to camp myself, I had received word from Quinn that he would not get his visa in time; I was crushed. But I did not worry. I was still going to see him at the end of the summer. I was going to live with my aunt while in England, and we would get our chance to really see where we could go. I had everything planned out; too bad I forget to tell God about those plans. It was about two weeks into camp that I received word from Quinn. Unfortunately, it was not the e-mail I hoped to receive. His e-mail informed me that he was sorry he was not there and how sorry he was that he had started to see a girl there at home. The rest of the words were a blur, and

I closed out my mail and just ran from the office. I am sure I received plenty of questioning looks, but I did not care. I did not stop until I got to the cabin. I was spending that summer rooming with Chelsea and Daisy—the best news I received when I arrived at camp. I just could not bring myself to utter the words to someone at camp just yet. Crying, I called Angie just so I would have someone to vent to. When I finally got myself together, I knew I still had to go to England just to prove to myself and ultimately everyone else that Quinn was not my only reason for going. This was something I really wanted to do. This just was not going to be my summer.

The only upside was that rooming with Chelsea and Daisy had made us like the three musketeers. Chelsea's birthday was coming up, and Daisy and I were determined to make it a special one. I needed the distraction. We got up early to decorate her area with balloons and signs. Needless to say, she was surprised and thrilled. I was glad we could put that smile on her face. Even when they had to separate us for a time during the summer, we ultimately found ourselves together again. We would spend our weekends off going to Chelsea's house with a group of friends. Even then, you couldn't separate us. I may have lost Quinn, but I had found the solid friendship with two girls that I just knew would last a lifetime. By the time camp came to an end, I was looking toward heading to England for my year abroad. It was not until the week before classes started at Liberty that I learned the paperwork and deposit for the program were never sent in. Now my problem was trying to figure out what I would do about school that coming fall.

# CHAPTER NINE

*Friends are treasures.*

*—Horace Burns*

As the start of the school year drew closer and closer, I found myself in a frenzy, trying to figure out what I would do. Did I skip a semester, take classes at home, or try to get into Liberty again? Angie and Chelsea were both starting their freshman year at LU, and I made sure to tell them about each other. My hopes were that if I could not be there for them, they could be there for each other. Little did I know that God was working in a way I never could have imagined.

I finally decided to go back to LU, and thankfully, I was able to get back in. While this was going on, I came to find out that Angie and Chelsea had found themselves in the same freshman seminar class, one sitting in front of the other. The connection was not made until Chels told the class what she did for the summer, and instantly, my prayer had been answered. Back home, I still had the problem of where I would be staying on campus. After talking with Chels, I found out she had an empty bed in her room. God had really been looking out for me. Before I knew it, I was back at Liberty, unpacking in a room that I was sharing with Chels and our other roommate, Linda. While I had originally felt that everything was falling apart, God showed me he had held it all together.

I found myself giving up on dreams. With the catastrophe that was Quinn, I had resigned to the belief that everyone else was destined to be happy and in love, and I was destined to be an old maid—the type of girl that guys saw as their friend or sister but did not see as someone they could fall for. I had always dreamed of getting married and starting a family. I looked around and saw what everyone else had and could not figure out why I was being left out of the equation. I had lots of questions and very few answers. To me, life was not fair.

As the semester began, Chels, Angie, and I were inseparable. Even though Angie was in a different dorm, she was conveniently only two buildings over. Whenever we could, we would find ourselves having meals together and spending our free time together. One night in particular, we were goofing off in our room and somehow we started to pretend we were sumo wrestlers. We were laughing so hard and making so much noise, the RAs from the floor below had our RAs coming in to find out what was going on.

With this now being my junior year, I found myself dealing with some of my tougher psychology classes and finding more free time proved to be more difficult. If there was one thing I had learned from the year prior, it was balance. Soon, I found myself, along with Chels, on hall leadership. After the previous year, I said I would not do it again. However, our hall was desperately trying to fill the spots, so I figured it could not hurt to give it one more try (mainly because it conveniently fulfilled my Christian service hours).

Chels was, of course, away from Ben again, and with it being her first semester, Ben decided to surprise her. Unfortunately, Ben said it was nearly impossible to surprise Chels—he obviously did not know me well enough. We decided to put a plan in motion to get him to Liberty. When he was finally able to confirm that he could come, we had it worked out that he would call about ten minutes before he normally did. I told Chels it was Tom that I was talking to, and she had high hopes of the two of us starting a relationship. She had no idea what was going on under her nose.

The day finally came for Ben to fly in. Since the airport in town was rather small, he had to fly into an airport an hour and a half away. He ended up missing his flight and had to catch a later one, meaning I had to miss one of my classes. I quickly had to come up with a reason for my being gone for three hours. Angie came to my aid. When it came time to pick up Ben, she called, and I gave Chels this sob story of how I had to go pick her up because she was stranded in that town. I told Chels I would be back by dinner. I picked Angie up, and I made a mad dash to pick up the roses Ben had requested and headed over to the restaurant and requested a table. Soon, Angie and I were on our way. Thinking we had arrived early at the airport, we found Ben outside waiting for us—his plane had come in early.

Soon we were on the road. I drove back to campus in hopes of not getting stopped for speeding. I was able to get Ben to where he would be staying and back to the dorm without Chels growing suspicious. By then, all she wanted to do was grab takeout and just have dinner in our room—something that had become a custom with us. Angie and I had to drag her out the dorm and to the restaurant. I stayed at the restaurant with Chels while Angie went back to pick up Ben. When they arrived, I excused myself to the restroom, leaving Chels sitting there by herself. Ben made his grand entrance, and the look on her face was priceless when she realized she had been had. The people around us started to applaud, many confusing the occasion for a proposal. Angie and I made our exit, but not before we received a glaring look from Chels. It felt good knowing I had made my friend so happy.

Like with everything, all good things must come to an end. It was time to take Ben back to the airport, and this time, Chels did that by herself. Ben, of course, had one more surprise up his sleeve. When she left, I went to get the roses he again requested and spread some of the petals on the bed and placed the bouquet and the note he left on her bed to be found when she returned. When she got back, I knew she had been crying. Needless to say, the flowers did not help that as she started to cry again when she saw them. I let her have a moment and then gave her a hug. I knew that as happy as she was to see him, it hurt to see him leave again. I could not help but wish I had a guy who evoked the same emotions from me.

Chels and I grew really close that semester—so close that we were hoping when we got married, we would at least live in the same town, if not the same neighborhood. We would stay up late into the night talking about our respective futures and our fears. We had even made a bet on who would be married first. The loser, the one who got married first, would make a speech at the winner's wedding reception about our bet. I was betting she and Ben would get married first—odds were kind of in their favor, but for the bet, the odds were in mine.

Halloween was upon us, and that meant one thing at Liberty: Scaremare. It was a haunted house of sorts, but inside they depicted scenes that would, at the end, result in the volunteers presenting the gospel. I had gone through when I was freshman, but the walls of the hallways they made were too close for my tastes, and I spent the entire time clinging to the back of Tom's shirt and periodically hitting buttons on my cell phone for some form of light. I vowed I would not go back. Somehow, Chels convinced me to go with a group from our dorm, Angie, and the brother dorm, which had affectionately deemed themselves the Brotel. We caught up with Eric, Patrick, and Ted and found ourselves going through as a group. Eric could have best been described as a big teddy bear, while Patrick was the guy all the girls made quick notice of, and Ted was the quiet one. While standing in line, we ran into Scott and Jeff. Jeff was in a class with Chels, so they too joined our group. Scott, a friend of Jeff's, was a tall goofball that made the time standing in line fly by. It was an experience I will not soon forget. By the time our group was up to head through, the girls were fully frightened and clinging to the back of Patrick. It was a nice way of introducing ourselves formally. Going through the house was not as bad as it had been the last time I was there, and before I knew it, we were in our tent, listening to our volunteer share with us. He recognized Scott, and soon we were having a good time of just sharing stories and laughing. I left knowing I probably would not go back again but glad I had gone this time. I made unsuspecting friendships with people that night, and that I would not give up for the world.

While Chels and I grew closer, a chasm was growing between Angie and me. I saw some of the choices she was making, and instead of being a good big sis like I should have and talked to her, I started to pull away. Before I knew it, I had put Chels between the two of us and the mini-war that was our friendship had begun. Eventually, I had completely shut Angie out. I found that I would spend my free time with Chels. I would not stop her from spending time with Angie, but when she would invite me to go along, I found I conveniently had work to do.

Without really trying, Chels and I had isolated ourselves from hall activities. We knew who our brothers were, but we tended to keep to ourselves. Even when we would have our meals, we would sit at the dorm tables but away from the others. Eventually, people just knew us as Chelsea and Becca—most not really knowing who was who. One day at lunch, we found ourselves being approached by Eric and Ted. That was the beginning of our coming out of our shells. Soon we found ourselves involved in more brother/sister activities and even at the guys' windows, talking into the late evening.

Still pretty fresh off the whole Quinn ordeal, I was finding that I could possibly have feelings for Eric. I was constantly going to God for guidance because I felt I could not take another heartbreak so soon. I tried to use Ted to feed me any information he could, but I was also afraid that if I were not careful, Ted might get the wrong idea. I was walking a thin line. It was coming to the end of the semester, and it had become pretty clear that Eric and I were destined to be just friends. No harm, no foul, and I did not end up with a broken heart—this time.

The guys in the Brotel were a bunch of pranksters. After some of the girls found their cars wrapped in plastic cling, we decided to strike back. The first was one of Eric's roommate's cars; next, we hit Eric's truck. We wrapped and wrapped and wrapped his truck in plastic cling, and for good measure, we stuck a tampon on the antenna—our proudest moment by far. If only we knew how badly they would retaliate.

Christmastime was fast approaching, and that meant two things: open dorms and Christmas break. For the first time in a while, I was excited about open dorms. The other times it was nice, but this time, I knew more guys would show up, and that made me happy. However, that day started off pretty badly. I had only four hours of sleep and four tests—you do the math. On top of all of that, it was raining. I was determined to have a good remainder of the day, despite how it had started. Chels and I had decorated our room with lights and ornaments, and Linda was gone for the night. We even had a sign up at the door that said "Free hugs and kisses"—of course implying the candy kind and not the real thing.

We went to dinner like we normally did and Chels asked if I could drive. We got to my car, and I was shocked to find a parking ticket on my car. It stated that I was not parked well enough in between the lines. I should have known something was up then. Instead, I was too outraged to think straight. By the time I pulled into the parking lot of the cafeteria (which the students had affectionately nicknamed the Rot), I was ready to call a lawyer. I had taken pictures before we pulled out to prove I was parked properly. It was about this time that as I was dialing to call my dad that I noticed Chels was laughing. I had been the subject of a prank by Eric and Ted. Apparently they got a hold of an old wet ticket with the prior writing gone and did their own handiwork. And to think my own roommate was in on it! I vowed to get them back. I did not know how, but I knew I would. That night at open dorms, I confronted Eric and Ted about their prank; they, along with Chels, just laughed. I found I could not be mad at them and soon found myself laughing right along with them.

I spent a lot of Christmas break talking to girls from the dorm and some of the guys from the Brotel. I even found myself on an emotional rollercoaster with one of the guys—one minute he wanted to take me out on a date, the next he was not sure as he was still hung up on another girl. After all I had been through with Quinn, you would think I had had enough. Apparently, I was a glutton for punishment. I was practically ready to run— run away from the problem as I had done many times in my life. Luckily, a friend helped snap me back into reality and helped me see that running only meant I had to deal with it later and I would not be happy. I decided that the new year would be different. I would not be afraid to love for fear of getting hurt. I would try new things; I would not be closed-minded. I soon found myself committing to spending time with Ted. I knew I had to be careful. I was not attracted to him, but I was attracted to the attention I was getting. I knew I should not settle, and I was acting shamelessly. At one point, he realized how different we were. I was relieved but also sad because I missed his sweetness. How shallow was I? Next thing I knew, he was confessing to liking me and wanted to know where things could go. I was falling for the idea of liking someone. I liked the idea of being in a relationship. If only I listened to myself.

When Chels and I returned from break, we found two major changes: Linda was gone, so now it was just the two of us, and we had crickets. We could not for the life of us figure out how that could be—we lived on the third floor! Soon, we found that other girls had crickets in their rooms as well. The Gabys—two girls with the same name who had become quick friends—were among the first to inform us of their plight. Gaby C, or GC for short, lived right next door to us and Gaby B, GB, lived on the other end of the hall. Christina, who lived across the hall from us, also had the same cricket problem. We were at a loss. It was not until Chels and I were talking to Eric and Ted via IM (instant messenger) that we discovered the source of our problem. They confessed, laughing, that during open dorms, they had guys from the Brotel bring paper cups (which at the time, we believed to have drinks in them) containing crickets on the hall and release the crickets in our rooms. Those crickets had been there for at least a month and were not leaving anytime soon. When we informed the other girls of how the crickets came to live with us, it would be an understatement to say that war on the Brotel was declared. We would have the last word in this one way or another. Now we just had to come up with how.

Being back at school, I realized that I did not see things going anywhere with Ted. We hung out enough in the few days before classes started—movies with the Brotel, hide and seek in DeMoss, and bowling—but I was not feeling the spark. I needed the spark. I found myself in one very confusing situation. Classes started, and I still did not have any romantic feelings for Ted. A month went by and still nothing. At the beginning of February, Chels invited a bunch of people from the dorm and Brotel to her house for the weekend. We all piled into two cars and set out for DC. It was a great weekend overall. It was at this time that the girls decided to inflict our revenge on the guys. For starters, after they had all fallen asleep downstairs, we quietly crept down the stairs to the basement. That was our headquarters, so to speak. We planned to pelt them with wet objects but not before we gathered some of their clothes and displayed them on the front lawn. The next morning, Chels's dad told the guys they may want to head outside to get their "decorations" off the lawn; it was by far the best prank. Needless to say, all of us girls locked ourselves in our rooms that night for fear of what would happen to us the next morning. The prank war had come to a cessation.

Valentine's Day was upon us, and Chels and I found ourselves in on a plan to set up a romantic first date for GC and Patrick. In the midst of the prank war coming to an end at Chels's, they made a connection. By then, I was rather jaded, and whole concept of Valentine's Day did not appeal to me at all. But this was for Gaby and Patrick, and that was what mattered. We set up a DVD player, blankets, ice cream, and candles at a park and sat and waited. By *we*, I mean Dane, Patrick's roommate, Ted, Chels, and I. Gaby and Patrick finally came, and we were off. By the time Gaby came back, she had a story that included half the candles being blown out by the wind, melted ice cream, and the police. Talk about your first date. After seeking as much advice from friends as possible, I had come to the conclusion that I did not really know Ted so I could at least give him a chance. We set up a date for that following weekend. I found myself going around still seeking advice, feigning that I was not sure what I should do. I knew one person I could go to and give me an honest answer—Tom. For that very reason, I was avoiding him because I knew he would tell me what I needed to hear. Deep down inside, I knew that I was asking for help so much because I wanted just one person to say don't do it. If I had only realized then that I did have one person saying don't do it all along: me.

The first date proved to be eventful. It started off going to one restaurant and ending up at a fast food place (very reminiscent of my first date ever.); the movie was great, but when we went back to the car, the key broke in the ignition. His roommate had to come bring us a spare. The best part was getting back to my room to find a bag with my favorite chocolates, favorite movie, and a mix CD; not bad, I figured. I was fighting not to run not too long after that. Before long, I was in a dating relationship with Ted. The shocker for most of my friends was that he was black. I had not previously dated a black guy. It wasn't that I was against it (I had my crushes), but remember, there was only one black guy in my high school, and everyone was trying to push us together. It was nothing serious, but still probably not the best idea considering my reservations at the beginning. I was still holding back, dealing with my own demons. I was living with the hurt and pain of guys past, and it was affecting my present. I could not look Ted in the eyes because somewhere along the way, I just could not look guys in the eyes period. I normally liked making eye contact with people.

120

Soon, Ted told me he loved me. I was getting ready to head for the figurative door at that point. We were not exclusively seeing each other, and I was still trying to figure everything out. Before I knew it, Ted officially asked and we were a couple. I wasn't dropping the *L* word anytime soon, and it frustrated him. Too much was happening too fast, and I took a day off from classes to sort everything out. I needed a day to clear my head and just get alone with God. I found myself sitting in a park, taking in the nature all around me. I needed something from God, and for me, nature was a good place to start.

When it started to rain, I made my way to a bookstore and spent the rest of the day there. I found myself walking the Christian book aisle, desperately seeking a sign from God. I came across *Extraordinary Faith* by Sheila Walsh, and it did not take long to realize that this was the book for me. I felt as if she had written my story and how I was feeling at the moment. I started to find my answers. I realized that like the author, after losing people I loved, I had come to the conclusion that it was not worth the pain of loving someone only to end up losing them in the end. I had a guarded heart, and my pain was so deep that I did not want to love again. Slowly, it became apparent that it was okay to love someone God had placed in my life. I just had to make sure that that person did not take God's place in my life.

I also realized that for so long, I felt that loving someone would result in them being taken by God from me. I did not have enough room for God and someone else, so I was "sacrificially" letting God have his place. I could not have been more wrong. The most startling of discoveries was that I was not living my life—I was living the life other people wanted me to live. I was living a life to avoid hurt and pain and ultimately that meant I was not living at all. I realized that I was being reminded of God's love. I was being reminded that life was full of disappointments, but that was only if my faith and trust was in man. God is immovable, dependable, trustworthy, and faithful, and banking on Him was something I could stake my life on. I had to be content with my current state and leave the rest up to God. That also meant realizing things would not always go the way I hoped or planned, but accepting that God knew best. By the time I got back to campus, I was a new me. I later discovered Ted had also taken the day to spend time with God. By the day's end, all was well in our relationship, but most importantly, all was well in my relationship with God.

Before I knew it, my junior year was coming to an end. Many changes had occurred in my life: I had a boyfriend, I had gained many new friendships with the girls on my hall, and Chels and I could not have been closer. The only downside was that I still had not patched things up with Angie. She had made previous attempts to contact me, but I would not give in to my stubbornness. It was not that Ted or Chels had not tried to get me to talk to her, but I was too stubborn and I was not ready to take that first step. While I knew I would be spending the next three months away from Ted,

I took solace in knowing that I would spend the summer at camp with Chels, Ben, Gaby, Patrick, and Daisy. I could not wait. Knowing Angie would also be at camp, I finally found myself contacting her and working out the problems in our friendship. That bit of drama did not compare to learning soon after that Ted was not coming back in the fall. All I could think was we would not get to celebrate our six-month anniversary as I had hoped. No double dates with Chels and Ben, as Ben would be starting that next semester at LU. I was also having problems with school financially and was just waiting for God to answer that prayer. With all this going on, I found myself worrying about the future. Everything was so uncertain and try as I might, trusting God completely was turning out to be harder than I ever imagined.

I came to find out that Ted would be taking classes during the summer while I was at camp. It was hard enough being so far apart, but now both of us would be busy, and that meant finding time to even talk would be difficult. On top of all of that, Ted was starting to doubt our relationship. He was feeling like second best, and there was nothing I could do to convince him otherwise. Sure I was interested in Eric first, but did it not count for something that I was with him? Soon I was realizing just how much of a roller coaster ride our relationship had started out as. By now, I figured we were more stable than we had started and that must mean all was well. On top of that, I found I was struggling with who I was. I was rooming with Chels and Gaby at camp, and I was finding it difficult to be with my two groups of friends. I was always teased about being "white," mainly because of the way I talked. Now, the whole issue of being "white" was starting to get to me, and I thought it was necessary to find my "black" side. This wasn't something I normally had to face. I was starting to feel like I was back in high school having to choose between two different groups of friends, and I didn't want to hurt anyone's feelings. In college, I experienced the same thing. Most of my friends were white, but at camp, I was encountering more and more black people. This wouldn't be a problem expect that the groups didn't really mingle unless they had to. This was something I saw at college and now was experiencing it at camp and honestly, I couldn't understand why that was. It didn't make sense why we all couldn't hang out together. It would be easier for me. I struggled all summer with that and found myself pushing away from my friends; I was depending more on Ted. He would help me find my "black" side, right?

Before long, summer had come to an end, and I was happy that Ted was going to come back that semester. I was soon back at LU—having to go back early for freshman seminar as a senior. Yeah, crazy, I know, but I never got to do it my freshman year, and my sophomore year I was told I would not be able to do it along with my leadership training; I soon found that was not true. All was not lost; Chels and I would be rooming together again with a freshman roommate. My senior year would be the best yet.

# CHAPTER TEN

*It is easy to dodge our responsibilities, but we cannot
dodge the consequences of dodging our responsibilities.*
—*Sir Josiah Stamp*

y senior year had finally started. I felt great.
Angie and I had patched things up, and she
was even living on the same hall as Chels and
I. Chels's sister, Claire, had also started her freshman
year at LU and was living on our hall. The Gabys had
returned as well, and I was feeling the love. Ben and Ted
were living on the same hall with the Brotel, and I would
be graduating that May. All was right in my world.

I found myself spending more and more time with
Ted and his friends and less with my own. When I asked
why we were not spending equal time with our friends,
he told me how my friends wore him out. Any right-
minded person would take that in offense and maybe end
the relationship—not me. While it hurt that he did not
want to spend too much time with my friends, I was okay
with it because I rationalized I would get to find myself.

I mean, I was in love, right? This was what God had for me, right?

Eric's sister, Carmen, was now attending LU and had found herself attracted to a tall guy named Marcus who was half-Cuban and half-black. She was so excited, and I, as her friend, was thrilled for her and encouraged her in any way I could. This sparked an argument between Ted and me. He felt that it was none of my business. He said I should not be getting involved in family affairs. That was the wrong thing to say to me. For once, I stood up for myself, saying she was my friend and came to me for advice and support. I am very much an advocate for interracial relationships, and he should've known that much about me by now. That was the one thing I would not back down on—not now, not ever.

Ted and I went to my house one weekend just to get away from campus for a bit. Leah was coming home that Saturday from a retreat that the school sponsored. She called my mom that Friday afternoon to inform her that she had sprained her ankle early that morning, or at least that is what the youth leaders told her. Mom was furious that they had not called her sooner and that they had given the phone to Leah to make the call. That Saturday when Mom went to pick her up, she watched in horror as Leah scooted on her rear end down the stairs of the travel bus. No one had offered to help her down off the bus. We could tell Leah was in pain, and as the day wore on, it was becoming more and more obvious that it was not just a sprain. Her ankle had more than doubled in size, and it was purple, black, and blue. Finally, we got her into the car and took her to the ER. Hours later it was confirmed that Leah broke her ankle and tore a ligament. My mom had gone past furious. To see the way that the people from our own home church had treated her daughter—it was on very few occasions that I had seen Mom this upset. It did bring up the question of race in my mind. Had it been anyone else's child, would they have gone about things in the same way? Hardly. We had learned over the years that because of the color of our skin, the church and the school somehow thought of us as less than human. We didn't deserve the same kind of respect because our skin color was darker than theirs.

We returned to school, and I found out later that week that Leah would be going into surgery to repair the ligament. I wanted to be home to be with my family, but my mom said that she would let me know when Leah came out and that I was not to worry. I found myself taking on anger for how my little sister had been treated. I know how it was for me going through that church and school, and it broke my heart to see how much worse it was for Leah. And the sad truth of the matter was that there were so many Leahs out there—so many kids that I knew I grew up with and so many that came through after us that were being treated differently because they did not have the right look or enough money or come from the right family. It was sad to think that so-called Christians would act that way.

Soon Ted and I were celebrating six months and talking of a possible future. After our past ups and downs, I learned not to push and tried to be in the moment. We had come to the point where we decided to focus on our friendship and not so much our relationship. I was struggling with my personal relationships, and I was struggling with my relationship with God. I was starting to wonder if there was something missing in my life. I had spent so much time around a certain group of people. I couldn't help but wonder what it would be like to step outside my box and explore the possibilities. I was still trying to keep worry at bay. Things were not turning out as I had hoped. I was so stressed out I was breaking out in little bumps all over. After two doctor's appointments, I was told I had a condition where my skin broke out due to stressful situations. I was given medication for it, but I knew the only real way to get them to go away was to stop worrying. Ted's parents were now in town, and I almost did not meet them. Ted had been protesting vehemently, and after much pestering, I was given the okay. I felt a little out of place, but eventually they made me feel at ease. It was important for me that his parents liked me. For some strange reason, I didn't know how to act around black people. To me it was almost a different culture. I don't say that to offend anyone, but I didn't grow up with pressure to be a certain skin color; I was taught to just be me. I was starting to see that for some, color was almost this stamp of pride. Whether you were black, white, Hispanic, whatever, the emphasis was solely on the color. Instead, shouldn't the emphasis of pride be on the culture? I just didn't know.

Our relationship was fragile to say the least. One Sunday we went out to eat and as the meal came to an end, I was asking the waitress for a to-go box for the rest of my meal. That resulted in Ted becoming upset with me, wanting to know why I could not eat all of my food in the restaurant. He was paying for it, so the least I could do was eat it all there; he asked why I was being wasteful. I couldn't believe him. It wasn't like I wasn't going to eat it. I just couldn't eat that much. Anybody who knew anything about me knew that. He kept asking why I couldn't be like Chels and Gaby who ate all their food. I had had enough. I didn't say anything but just left. I soon found myself desperately trying to eat everything on my plate the times we went out to eat just to avoid getting yelled at again. There was one time we were out with friends and I actually looked at him, apologetically, because I couldn't finish my food. Sometimes, I just would not get much to eat at all and then he wanted to know what was wrong; really?

I shortly found myself having to be careful in things I said around Ted. My sense of humor did not seem to be funny to him, and it was getting to be like walking on eggshells. The time I spent with Chels and Angie had grown to be less and less. Chels knew something was up and called me on it. We got into an argument, and need-less to say, she put me in my place. I was not upset with what she had said—I missed having someone giving it to me straight like Tom did. I just didn't know how to tell her what I was feeling inside and what was going on with me. I was struggling with my identity and I didn't think she would understand. I also didn't want to admit how things were truly with Ted or how they had been—it would be like admitting failure. I left the room and sought out Angie. She seemed to get what I was saying, even if she didn't understand it completely. Eventually, I decided I needed to move out. Partly, it was to find myself and partly, it was due to the fact that I had learned I didn't have enough money to finish my last semester. I was also struggling to get along with our other roommate. Moving off campus seemed to be the solution to my problems. I was running away from my problems like I always had, but the only thing it did was create more.

Christmas break arrived, and I was struggling with all the craziness in my life. I had to move and find an apartment, but at least I had found a roommate. Ted wasn't coming back and soon we found ourselves not in a relationship anymore. Chels still did not know what was going on, and we were not talking. Frankly, I was just ready to graduate. I was finally able to get things worked out to move off campus and was moving into a great place. I was also hoping my roommate would help me find my black side. Since I had spent the majority of my life with white friends, to me this was a necessity. Like I said, it was a different culture, and since I am black, I figured that I had to find out why it was different. My culture and heritage, West Indian, is about being proud of who you are and the things that make you unique. The focus isn't on the color of your skin. Unlike here in the States, just because you're black, that doesn't automatically make you African American. To be honest, my family doesn't claim that. Our ancestors aren't just from Africa nor do they make up the majority. The Arawak and Carib Indians (the original inhabitants of the islands) make up that majority with influences coming from England, France, and Spain. I'm not saying that slavery didn't happen in the islands, but it wasn't like here in the States. People make assumptions because of the color of your skin and don't bother to ask. They read their history books and take things for granted. I just wanted to know what it meant to be black in the United States.

When I returned that semester, I got my stuff and moved. Chels still wasn't back, so I left a note explaining my situation and why I had to move. Needless to say, that didn't go over well. We had a class with Eric, and he had to be a buffer between the two of us because of all the tension. I thought I was in heaven off campus. All my problems had ceased—well, almost all of them. With Ted back home, we found ourselves in an on-again, off-again relationship. He had one of his good friends keeping tabs on me, making sure I was okay and things went well for a while. Before long, I found my own apartment suffocating. My roommate had people over all the time and at all hours. I was finding it difficult to study. I even found myself heading back to Angie's dorm room to find peace and quiet. How ironic, as that was one of the reasons I left in the first place.

While my semester was seemingly falling apart, I received word of what would be the highlight of my academic career that April. Earlier in the semester, I learned via e-mail that I was up for the student achievement award, given to seniors who excelled in academics and extracurricular activities. I was surprised, as I was wondering how I registered on their radar. I was one of five nominees, and I could think of many others who deserved to be nominated above me. I was flattered, to say the least. It proved to me that you just never know who is watching you. While I didn't win that award, I got to share that night and experience with my family and Angie. By now, I was seeing how dumb I had been in handling the whole situation with Chels and hoped she could share that day with me. Unfortunately, she was out of town for a youth convention that same weekend. I figured it was just as well as she probably wouldn't have wanted to come. I couldn't really blame her. If she hated me for the rest of my life, I wouldn't have batted an eye, as I knew I hated myself for it all.

I found myself wondering if I had made a bad decision when it came to my choice in major. I liked psychology and all, but deep down inside, I could not shake my love for science and ultimately wanting to be a doctor. I was starting to see that maybe it was just too late for me. I made an appointment to meet with my favorite psychology professor, Dr. G, and discuss my options. He told me that he knew of psychology students who had gone on to medical school and that the only thing they really had to do was take the necessary science classes that were requirements to get into medical school. He told me if it was something I really wanted to do, I could and that I needed to realize it would take time. With it being my last semester, in my last year, I knew that would mean taking more classes even after I graduated. Was it something I really wanted? Was it something I wanted to put the time into doing? I knew at that point that only time would tell.

My roommate and I eventually grew apart, and we were just two people living together. The same friend that Ted had keeping tabs on me found my roommate and her friends more interesting, and I found myself feeling more and more lonely. One day, she came by and I pretended not to be home. I could not take her not acknowledging my presence. When my roommate got home, there was Ted's friend yelling and cursing at me right behind my roommate. Somehow, the yelling turned to hitting and scratching, and I found myself using my arms to block my face from being scratched off. My roommate finally pulled her away and told her to leave. I was furious. I did not want that girl back in my apartment. My roommate soon left, and I was all alone.

Ted was soon calling and IM'ing me, telling me it was all my fault; talk about the straw that broke the camel's back. It was bad enough I had found myself in the situation I was in, but having Ted, who was miles away, telling me I was all to blame hurt like no other pain. He said he had gotten all the facts from his friend and my room-mate. While my initial actions were childish, that did not give her the right to act like she did. Now he was telling me I was disinvited from the trip to his hometown after graduation. I was the troublemaker in all this, and I just needed to go away. I could not take it any longer. I called Angie and told her what happened. She came over to comfort me, but I was still feeling all alone. After she left, I knew I needed time away from the situation. I packed a bag and headed home. I needed to be somewhere where I knew I was loved. My apartment and school were not the place, considering that those who loved me for me I had long since pushed out of my life. What was I going to do? I was doing the only thing I knew how to do best: run.

I finally found myself at home and just praying no one would try to find me. I needed time to think and I just needed to know I was loved. My mom was not too happy to discover I had picked up some injuries during my scuffle, but I was just happy to be home. While my plan was to eventually get back to school by that follow-ing Tuesday, all that changed when Dad discovered my car was not drivable. After taking it to a body shop, I was dismayed to find I was stuck until it got fixed. On the other hand, I was relieved to not have to head right back. Before long, people were starting to ask questions about where I was. Scott had somehow gotten informa-tion from Angie about what happened and was ready to come to my defense and aid if I needed it. That day he solidified a place in my life forever.

Somewhere along the way, Scott and I had become really good friends, even though he was now living in Kentucky. When we first met, if anyone had told me we would be good friends later down the road, I honestly would have laughed at them. Chels had even asked Angie what happened to me, as I was not in class. I had already informed my professors of the situation and that I was doing as much as possible to get back. If anything, graduation was less than a month away! Even Ted finally located me, though he had to ask my sister. I found it odd that the one person who seemed to care less was my roommate.

Days turned to weeks and eventually, it was almost a full month before I could return, just in time for exam week. While I was able to fulfill the majority of my assignments at home, I had some problems with two of my classes. One of the professors refused to let me make up the final. The other, since it was an online class, had no idea I was taking the class—apparently, I was the only one enrolled in the class. Long story short, I was not able to take the exams. Everything was falling apart in my world. I had my family and my faith, yet I felt utterly alone. To top it all off, I found I had been gaining weight from the stress of it all. Try as I may to exercise and watch what I ate, the weight kept coming on.

Graduation was soon upon me and to compound on an already bad situation, I discovered none of my brothers were going to be able to make it to my college graduation. It was my second significant graduation in my life, and it was turning out to be like nothing it was supposed to be. Like the first, it was starting off like a nightmare. I enjoyed the ceremony with my friends and what family that were able to assemble. I walked across the stage, smiling and grateful for the past four years, regardless of the past few months. In a few days, I would be off on vacation with the same girl who tried to rearrange my face and the same ex-boyfriend who constantly found every way to belittle me; boy, was I a glutton for punishment.

The summer came and went, and I discovered I did not graduate after all. I was short the credits from those two particular classes I had problems with and I spent that summer fighting it with appeals. With all of this going on, I was trying to reach out to Chels. She, Ben, Daisy, and Eli were spending their last summer at camp. Daisy and Eli were engaged to be married, and I knew Chels and Ben's engagement would be coming soon. After sending a note to her at camp, begging for forgiveness, Chels wrote back that she had already forgiven me, but that it would take time to get back to where we were. That was probably the best news I could have gotten and a lot more than I felt I deserved. I hoped that in time God would repair our friendship, and I prayed that it would be soon. I desperately missed my Chelsea.

In other areas of my life, I was still in contact with Alex and we felt that our lives were paralleling each other. She was in an on-again, off-again relationship with a guy she knew would come back after pushing her away. Ted and I were talking again and were even giving it another shot. A few days later, as I was talking to him online, I was stunned when he told me it was not working. In fact, he wanted nothing more to do with me. After going through the rollercoaster of one day wanting to be with me and the next not, I wasn't hurt; I was mad. I was tired of this seesaw that benefited him and him alone. I had to do it all on his time and when it best suited him. I was finally tired of it. I did not fight. I just let him go, knowing that it would be only a matter of time before he would be asking to be back in my life. He always did.

After many appeals, I finally was able to get a meeting before the student council. I was going to get my chance to get my degree I worked so hard for. I knew now that psychology was me taking the easy way out and that deep down, I wanted to be a doctor. I wanted to go to medical school. I just needed my degree. The day for me to meet before the council finally came, and I found myself back at LU. While my family was able to come into the meeting, I knew that all of the talking was up to me. Before about ten or so of the school's heads of various departments, I told my story. Eventually, it came around to my car breaking down and why I left town in the first place. For the first time, I let someone outside of my family and very few select friends know of my assault from a so-called friend. When asked why I did not call the police or campus security, I finally told what no one had known but me. Knowing that this "friend" had already been held by the police for a previous altercation and that she had described herself as the attackee, I felt as though I would have been the one to get into trouble. Not to mention, my roommate was siding with her and it would have been two against one. I wouldn't have stood a chance. After hearing my side of things, I was informed that I would be receiving their decision by mail. I walked out of the room knowing that whatever happened, it was up to God and the few people in that room.

With all that was happening, it did not take long for me to hear from Ted. It had only been a few months since he had told me he wanted nothing more to do with me. Now he was back saying he needed my friendship. This time, I was on my guard. I desperately wanted to say "No, leave me alone," but I couldn't; I believe in giving people second chances. I said it was fine, but I was keeping him at arm's length. He had hurt me so much in the past year, and I was not going in blindly this time.

It did not take long for me to hear back from the council that I would be able to take a withdrawal from both classes and if I wanted, I could take the online class free of charge considering the circumstances that surrounded that class. I could take classes at home to fill the other requirement. I was ecstatic! Finally, I could see a little light in this dark hole that had become my life. I took the necessary classes, passing with two As and a B, and I was able to graduate in May of the following year. Since I had walked the previous May, I did not feel it necessary to do it all again. I had what was important: my degree.

My twenty-fourth birthday was drawing near, and there was something that was pressing on my mind. I was tutoring an old family friend in high school calculus, and every time I went to his house, I would pass the cemetery where Will was buried. Since his passing, I had not been to his grave, but I made up my mind that before I turned twenty-four, I would go visit his grave and say my final good-bye. The day arrived, and I took the time necessary to go to the grave site before any of my other duties started calling my name. When I pulled up, I wasn't sure exactly where his grave was, but all I knew was that it was close to the front.

I did not have to walk far to find his headstone. It seemed so odd to see his name written on the headstone there in the ground; maybe I was still waiting for someone to wake me up from what had to be a dream. I stood there for a minute thinking of all the things I wanted to say. I think that I had not been to his grave up to that point because I was mad at him. I was mad that he left like he did; I was mad because who was going to be the Spanky to my Buckwheat? There seemed to be a hundred questions but no answers because he was not there to give them. I spoke my mind and told him how I missed him and that I looked forward to the day when I would see him again. Somewhere in that space of time, I got a sense of peace. I needed to do that on that day. It was letting go of a piece of my past and moving forward into my future. I knew that Will would never be forgotten in my mind. I left an artificial yellow rose on his headstone—my last tribute to my friend. I turned and walked back to my car, looking forward to what the next year would have for me.

It was shortly before graduation that I received the devastating news that Jerry, the cofounder and chancellor of Liberty, was gone. I cried like I hadn't in a long time, not wanting to accept the reality of it all. I called Angie to find out how everyone was taking the news, and she said it was as though campus had turned into a ghost town. She was also in shock and disbelief, half expecting to hear he was okay. If there was one thing about Jerry, it was that he had a twenty-year plan and he was nowhere near finishing it. He just could not be gone. I finished my conversation with Angie and continued calling friends to see how they were doing and if they knew. That even included a call to Ted. When Dad learned I had called him, he wanted to know why I had called "that jerk." Now normally, as far as I knew, my dad had not said much about my dating life. To hear him say that made me feel so loved and so good because I knew he knew, even if I did not tell him. In his own way, my dad was looking out for me. Even on a sad day as it was, I had found a silver lining.

# CHAPTER ELEVEN

*Assert your right to make a few mistakes. If people can't accept your imperfections, that's their fault.*
—*Dr. David M. Burns*

The summer came, and I was working in a doctor's office. I needed money for school, and this would hopefully help. Before long though, I was facing another problem: my right knee, which I had injured in high school, was acting up. Eventually, I was in so much pain that the only way for me to get around was on crutches. I was soon seeing my doctor and eventually off to see a specialist where I learned that I had a dislocated knee cap. I went through a few weeks of physical therapy in hopes that it would help the pain. If it didn't work, I would be off to surgery. Physical therapy was painful. I started off not knowing if I would make it through to the end. I was able to do my therapy at home and I had to do it two times a day, but I was working to improve the condition of my knee. It did not help that I was at the heaviest I had been probably in all of my life. After the prescribed time had passed, I was starting to feel much better. This news meant one thing: I was to continue my therapy.

In this time, when life to me was practically standing still, Chels and Ben were now engaged; Angie had found the love of her life, and Daisy and Eli were now married. Chels and I were steadily patching things up, and I was delighted to find I was invited to her bridal shower. My family and I had already received our save the dates, and I was just honored that they would even want me there with all that happened. I set out the weekend of the shower with high hopes. Chels and Angie were now sharing an apartment off campus with another girl, so I would be staying with them. Angie knew I was hoping to get a chance sometime that weekend to have a talk with Chels and hopefully try to explain some things. I was nervous and just not sure how it would all go.

I was able to spend some time with Carmen during my visit. Somewhere along the way, we had become great friends. God knew I needed someone like her in my life. She was normally the one I called when I needed encouragement. She was the one I called when I needed to just hear how good God was. In spite of all that had happened, I knew God was working in it all and was working it out for my good. Seeing Carmen and getting to spend time with her was just what I needed and proof of that very fact.

The shower was great, and I even won the "who knew Chels best" game. Chels's parents were in town, and I got to see them. All was going well. The next day, I knew we would all be spending time together. By we, I mean Chels,

Ben, Angie, her boyfriend, Aidan, and myself. When Ben came over, he wrapped me in a hug and we just held on for a little bit. It had been a while since we had seen each other, and that hug meant a lot. There was forgiveness and hello and just so much; I found myself tearing up in that moment. I felt that my extended family had been rebuilt. The time we spent together was uneventful. I felt like things were finally getting back to normal; it felt like old times and that nothing had changed. Maybe, just maybe, this really was my identity after all.

Later that night as Chels got ready for bed, Angie "gently" nudged me to talk to Chels. I had been waiting all weekend to talk to her; it was now or never. I went in and after fumbling a bit, I finally got out the words I hoped would provide some explanation. I knew there was a lot to tell her, but I just asked again for forgiveness and told her how terribly sorry I was. After a while, we talked about her upcoming wedding and her plans, and I felt as though things would be back to normal. I felt as though I had my Chels back. Things were looking up.

After my great weekend with my "extended family," it was back to the grind of work. I soon heard from Ted again. He had sent me a text message to call him. It was just as I was about to call that I stopped myself, realizing that no matter what, things would never change. He would always want to communicate on his terms. I simply replied that if he had something to say or ask, he could call. I knew in that instance we could no longer be friends. Our dynamic was toxic. It would always be him determining when and how we communicated. It would always be on his terms. It had always been and would always be what was convenient for him. He was only looking out for himself, and it was time I looked out for myself. I was always concerned with how things affected us, and he was more concerned with how things affected him. I knew I needed friends who encouraged me, loved me and accepted me for me, and knew I did the same for them, no matter their skin color or heritage. With Ted, I was starting to realize I would never get that. I finally did what I should have done a long time ago. I informed Ted I no longer wanted anything to do with him. I told him how it was best for us both. All we did was continue in this harmful cycle, and it would not end until I ended it. I knew that in the long run, he would see it as being for the best. I didn't want him to try to contact me in any way because I would not respond. I was finally able to *really* let go of something I should not have started in the first place.

The weekend of Chelsea and Ben's wedding approached. The day we were planning to leave, Dad woke up sick and informed us he could not go. In order for us to get down there, I would have to drive; I was nervous. It was not that I was afraid to drive the distance, but rather the night before I had only about five hours of sleep in anticipation of the next day. Also, there was not the option of not going. Angie was riding with us, and the maid of honor had to get to the wedding. I drove Mom, Leah, Angie, and myself the nine hours to Hattiesburg. When we arrived, Angie called to let them know we were there. Claire informed her she was on her way to pick us up. The nerves were rising again. I thought it enough that we had been invited, and the last thing I wanted was to get in the way of the activities of the bridal party. Claire and her cousin arrived, and Angie and I were off to wherever everyone else was. We got to the place where pretty much family was staying, and it was kind of a camp reunion. With many of Chels's relatives being there, along with Daisy and Eli, I did not feel too out of place. The odd moments came when people assumed I was in the bridal party. I just had to smile and say I was not, and I knew that it was my fault. Near the end of the gathering, we kidnapped Chels for her bachelorette party. This just involved ice cream at a local restaurant, but so many of us crammed into an SUV with the bride-to-be was the best part. The evening came to an end, and I was being dropped off at the hotel alone. With the bridal party all staying together elsewhere, it was again a reminder of my mistake. I just prayed to get through the remainder of the weekend.

The day of the wedding finally arrived, and I could not have been happier to get to watch two people who loved each other so much finally get married. I knew that if I could find a fraction of what they have, I would consider myself truly blessed. The ceremony was beautiful, with Ben busting out his own vows, much to everyone's surprise. The reception was wonderful as we soon found ourselves all together again. I knew that Chels and Ben were truly glad we were there. I knew all was in the past and forgiven—at least they had forgiven me. After a few dances, we sent the newlyweds off on their honeymoon, knowing we would see each other soon enough—for Angie's wedding in two months.

After coming home from Chels and Ben's wedding, I had come to realize that while I knew God, Chels, and all had forgiven me, there was one person left to forgive me—me. I felt ashamed of how I acted. I felt ashamed of the relationship I had with Ted and how I let that influence and affect other parts of my life. Somewhere along the line, I let myself lose myself. I pushed my life aside to be a part of his life. I was guilty of pushing aside the ones that really knew me and loved me for something that I thought was better. Ultimately, I was ashamed that I didn't have the courage to tell one of my closest and dearest friends what was really going on. I had spent so much time with the guilt, and while I am by no means perfect, I knew I had to cut myself some slack. Everyone makes mistakes, and it is important to learn from them. I just had to stop dwelling on them. It was time I forgave myself and allowed myself the chance to move on and grow in the wake of all that happened. I was holding myself prisoner to my mistakes, and I alone held the key to my freedom. With God's help, I began to heal. I began to heal not only from my mistakes but also from the hurt and pain I had been put through. While no one asked for forgiveness or saw anything they had done against me as wrong, I knew I had to forgive them in my heart so that bitterness and anger did not take hold. With all of that weight off my shoulders, I was finally starting to feel alive again.

Angie and Aidan's wedding was soon upon us. Before I knew it, I was in Greenville sharing a room with Chels, Ben, and Claire. Some might think this whole setup as being a little weird, but after all the weekend trips to Chelsea and Claire's during camp, this was just another big sleepover. The day of the bridal luncheon, I gave Angie a gift. The same scrapbook she had given to me when I turned sixteen and then revamped when I turned eighteen, I gave back to her. I added photos of her and Aidan and told her it was now something we would pass back and forth for the rest of our lives on significant occasions. I was not really expecting the tears that followed, but her mom thought that it was a great idea. I do believe our sisterly bond was sealed for good that day.

Soon their wedding day was here, and I was feeling insecure as my weight had me feeling less than lovely in my bridesmaid dress. I just wanted to be there for Angie and make it through the day without embarrassment. The ceremony was performed by her dad, and it was lovely, even though I fidgeted through the whole thing. My shoes were killing me and by the time we all got back into the hallway, they were off and I was giving myself a much-needed break. Thankfully, I discovered I was not the only one suffering from shoe problems. Some of the other bridesmaids were talking of their feet hurting and removing their shoes when they got the chance. The reception was beautiful even if it took a while for the bride and groom to get a ride to the hotel—they couldn't find the car keys. When it came time for the bouquet toss, I was up front with Claire (who was getting married only a few months later) and Angie's roommate from college. At Chels's wedding, she had tried to get it to me, but her cousin got to it before I did. This time, Angie made sure I was in prime position to catch it. Front and center, I got ready, knowing I had never caught one of these in my life. Angie let the bouquet fly. Arms up, I caught the bouquet and started wondering if the sentiment behind it was true. I guess I would have to wait and see. After making a few rounds to say hello and good-bye to friends, I bid Angie and Aidan farewell, and Chels, Claire, Ben, and I walked out to leave. I got my stuff from their car and my parents pulled up as I said good-bye. I told Ben that I only hoped that whoever I married got along well with him. Part of me wanted to explain why I had said that, considering all that occurred with Ted, but I felt it best to just leave it be. We said our good-byes, only hoping to be together again soon.

In that time frame, I left the church that I had spent the past seventeen or so years in, and I branched out and found my own church. In my search, I prayed that God would show me a place where I knew instantly I belonged. I went to a few, but they reminded me too much of the church I was in previously. I found one not too far from where I was living, and I prayed that if it was the place for me, three people would say hello to me. I took Leah with me, and we had not even made it to the door before seven people had welcomed us and told us how glad they were to see us. I knew instantly that I had found my new church home.

While I loved my new church, I was feeling somewhat lonely. I prayed that God would provide a friend for me. When I met Cynthia, she was not exactly the type of friend I was looking for. She was older than I—a grandmother to be exact—but there was something about the way she treated me that I could not easily dismiss her friendship. I had no idea how God would use her in a few months time to help me over one of the biggest hurdles I would face to date.

A few months had passed, and one night, I found myself at home alone with Leah. I had just eaten a piece of pineapple and feeling guilty (I had reason to believe I was allergic to cooked pineapple), I panicked. All types of scenarios were running through my mind. I went looking for my inhaler, but I did not have it; Mom did. I called Dad on his cell phone, but I could not get a hold of him.

Before I knew it, my heart was pounding in my chest. I thought I was having a heart attack or something. Leah called 9-1-1 and eventually got a hold of my parents. We just told them to meet us at the hospital. By the time the ambulance got there, I felt I would have been better off driving myself considering we were only five minutes from the hospital. After a few hours in the ER, it was ruled that I had had a panic attack. The next week included two more trips to the ER. After three EKGs, a chest x-ray, and many blood tests, they could not find anything wrong with me. I scheduled an appointment with my regular doctor, praying that God would give him wisdom and that I would get some answers. After he looked at all the results from the various tests I had done at the hospital, he ruled that I was stressed. I told him a list of other things that I was experiencing, and he said it was all because of stress.

I could not have been more relieved. With all that had happened in the past two years, it was no wonder where my stress came from. He advised that I get on with my life and start losing some weight. I had literally holed myself up, too ashamed of how I looked. I knew that all the weight gain had been from stress, but hearing it from the doctor's mouth made it all the more official. I left that day determined to reduce my stress level and to start living my life. It took a while for me to start living again, and I found myself in church one Sunday telling Cynthia of what happened. I soon discovered that she too had experienced panic attacks and knew exactly what I was going through. God had not only provided me with a friend, but a friend that I needed for that particular time in my life.

# CHAPTER TWELVE

*We are meant to learn from our yesterdays, not live in them.*

—*Rebecca Thomas*

It is months later, and I am happy to say my stress level has gone down and I have lost a considerable amount of weight. I have learned so much. If anything, my faith has gone to a deeper level. Going through the few weeks after the panic attack, I had to learn to rely on God to be my strength and sanity. Every day was a struggle because in the back of my mind was this great fear that it would all happen again and it could be so much worse. The fear had paralyzed me in such a way that it was stifling. I desperately wanted the life that I had back, and it seemed that it would take forever. I guess that is where one of my first lessons came in—learning to be patient. That definitely has not been one of my strong points, and realizing that I now had to take everything one day at a time for my own health forced me to step back and just breathe. I had to be able to just take it one thing at a time and accept that it would not all come back in a day.

The fear was threatening to take so much from me, but I am a fighter and the fear was not going to win. I had to set in my mind that no matter what, each day with God's help, I would awaken to see the new day for what it was—an opportunity to be the person I may not have been the day before. My faith was what kept me going in those first few days after the panic attack. I realized that all my life I had been struggling with fear and worry. So many times I found myself giving situations over to God, but for some reason no sooner had I given it to him, I was taking it right back. Did I honestly think I could do a better job with the situation at hand by worrying over it? Yeah, right. Still, this principle did not really take hold until I learned that I did not need to know the why behind everything. In my scientific brain, I had to know why things happened and how they happened. It was not until I realized and accepted that I could not logically understand *everything* that I was able to let go of more and worry less. Mercifully, God gently and sometimes not so gently, would remind me that I needed to give the situation back to Him to handle and to rest in Him.

I can honestly look back now and be thankful for the whole experience of it all; and I do mean everything. I know that sounds crazy, but it all gave me back my self-worth and my sense of self. For so long I thought I had to be one thing or another or that I had to compromise who I was to fit in. All the wrong friends I made along the way that tried to belittle me or tried to hold me down or keep me back from achieving my dreams; those few I have come to realize were just afraid. To me, it seems that most people are afraid to dream and those same people are afraid of those who dare to dream. The fear of those daring few is rooted in that they are willing to try to do what many others would dare not. I dream and I dream big. I still struggle day to day with it all, but I know I am not a quitter and that I am more determined than ever to reach for my dreams.

I realized that my desire to be a doctor was not really mine. I took what I thought was a sign in a certain period of time in my life as the answer to that burning question: what do I want to be when I grow up? I made a decision in haste, under pressure, and with little thought and held on to it as though it were a dream. I have since realized that sometimes God will pry open our closed grasp on things to get us to realize what is really out there for us. I have since let go of that dream to be a doctor, but not without a lot of agony. I was constantly wondering what everyone would think, what would I say to all the questions—again, I found myself more worried about everyone else and forgetting about asking what I want. So what do I want? I want to be happy; I want to be proud of what I am doing; I want to make a difference. Since writing this book, it has taken some time, but I have gone back to school. Not because I have to, but because I want to. Writing this book opened a door I did not know existed for me. I discovered a passion that had been sleeping deep down inside for years. I had made previous attempts when I was in high school to write books, but I was not really serious about it so I never finished. This time, I did finish and I found something I truly love.

I hope that everyone gets the opportunity at least once in their lifetime to find that thing that makes them feel truly alive.

It took a while, but finally I realized that the person I had been all along was the person that my true friends loved. They never asked me to be anything more or anything less than I already was. For a while, I bought into that whole idea that skin color was what made you who you were. They weren't concerned with the color of my skin. It is a shame that it took almost losing all of them for me to finally realize that. I also found that for so many years I was unhappy with the way I looked. I thought I had to be one shape or size to be loved and accepted. It took stress and a panic attack for me to realize that I was beautiful just the way I was. When I was at my heaviest, I found that I loved the person that I was the most. I realized I was not perfect, but at the same time, I was still beautiful. It finally dawned on me that I was beautiful, not because of what I looked like on the outside, but because of who I was on the inside. When that shines through, the outer beauty is magnified. I deserve the best, and I refuse to settle for less than that in any aspect of my life. When I finally started to accept that, the stress and weight came off in leaps and bounds. Society, whether it is our magazines, TV shows, friends, families, or in my case, even church groups, has us thinking that the only way to be beautiful is to be a certain size. If there is one thing I have learned, I do not look good as a size two or four. I look like I am malnourished and could use a cake or two to help put on some weight. Everyone is different, and it is in those differences that there is true beauty. I digress from that as I could go on and on with this subject.

In the past three years that I have been single (and yes, I still am, and I am happy), I realized that I learned so much about myself and even relationships that I do not think I would have learned had I been in a relationship. In looking back over all my crushes and relationships, I realized that most of the time, I found I could compare myself to the main character in the movie *Runaway Bride*. If you have never seen the movie, the basic premise is that she is a bride who has run out on all three of her weddings just as she is walking down the aisle. A reporter comes in to rewrite a previous story he had written about her and ends up falling in love with her. This time, she leaves her current groom at the rehearsal and realizes she has fallen in love with the reporter. Unfortunately, she leaves the reporter at the altar as well. While gathering research for his story, the reporter uncovers that in each of her previous relationships, the bride was always into the activities of her groom but did not have an identity of her own. When all is said and done, she does end up marrying the reporter, but not before she discovers who she really is. Looking back, I realized that I was doing the same thing. I was trying to meld into what I thought most of these guys wanted, and I ended up losing who I was along the way.

I have given up on the whole idea of a "man of my dreams." Wait and hear me out before you think I have completely lost it. I have had way too much time to sit and think of what the ideal guy for me would be like that he finally became too perfect. If I had to look for a guy that measured up to him, I would find myself constantly being disappointed. I have come to realize that there are only a few things that are really important in the guy for me. As long as he loves God, his family, loves and accepts me for me (and has to at least understand why I love Duke so much. Just kidding—sort of.), I will be happy.

I discovered along the way that I am not looking for a fairytale ending. I will look for a love to last a lifetime. I realize that I cannot rely on feelings; they are constantly changing. I know with my own family that there are days I love them and there are days I start to wonder if I am adopted. I accept that whomever I may get to share my life with, there will be days I will love them and there will be days I may contemplate murder. Each day will be a new day to determine in my heart and mind that I will love this person, for better or worse. It is about loving an imperfect person imperfectly, but completely. Now, have I been in love? I do not have to be in love to know what love is. You see, I have a family that loves me no matter what, who has been there for me through thick and thin, and has supported me in all my endeavors. I have seen what my parents have had to endure for me to be where I am today and I know it took a lot of sacrifice. I know there is no way I could ever repay them for all they have given and all the love they have bestowed on me. My mom especially is my hero. Not that I do not love my dad for all he has done, but when it comes to who has fought for me more when it comes to injustices, Mom wins hands down. I have seen her fight when someone has tried to belittle her children. I can only hope and pray that if I become a mother, I am half as great as she is. I have friends that, no matter what I may have put them through, have stuck by my side and still love me. So again, I ask, have I been in love? My answer is that I am one of those imperfect people who has been loved imperfectly but completely, and I am thankful for that fact.

With all of that said, I will admit that I do struggle with the idea of a husband and family because I feel that for me, there is so much more to life. I do not want to be that person that gets married, has kids, and that is it, and that is what you are supposed to do. For some, this means success. They have accomplished being successful in their life endeavors. They have the job, the spouse, the kids—what more could they ask for? Do not get me wrong; I have friends that feel that their life is complete by being a wife and mother, and they are truly happy. For me, however, that would not make me feel complete. To me, there is so much more to life. I want my life to matter, and I want to make a difference in the lives of the people I encounter. I do not want to just live because that is what I am doing; I want to live because of passion and the reality that life is short and we are to make the most of every day we are given. It is not something I have completely ruled out as a possibility, but it also is not a priority in my life as of right now. It just means that my definition of success is different, and that's okay. There is more than one definition for success.

I am glad to say that all of my girls have found their Prince Charming, and I know they are loved. I still keep in close contact with Chels, Angie, Alex, Carmen, Tabby, and Daisy. It has taken me this long to only start to wonder why I get along so well with these girls and why I depend heavily on them and trust them so. I realized it is because we are so much alike. I spent so much time seeing all the differences and what they could do better than me that it never dawned on me what we had in common. Chels and I both struggle with worry. I would have never known! I always saw her as someone that was well put together, had everything under control, and that made me look up to her; I thought that she did not have a worry in the world! I laughed when I realized that it was quite the contrary. Like me, she worries about everything, and that only makes me love and respect her more.

Angie and I struggled with self-perception—wanting to look perfect. It took realizing that perfection is only a concept and that we had to be happy with what we had. It may not be perfect, but it is good enough, and frankly, we love what we have. We both plan on getting that bikini that for so many years we kept putting off because this was wrong or that was wrong. We have God-given curves, and we love them. With Alex, it is our love-hate relationship over basketball. We always say we will be old women sitting in the stands at the yearly Duke-UNC games, cheering on our respective teams and still ribbing each other about who is better. She is also my dose of confidence. It never fails that in talking with her, I will always feel better about myself. She is confident in who we are, and make no mistake about it, she will let you know. She brings out the best in me, most of the time, and I am thankful for her.

Carmen is still my go-to girl when I need to be reminded of just how good God really is. We both struggle with leaving things in God's hands but always encourage each other to do it, no matter how hard it may be. We encourage each other to keep going, no matter how tough things may get because in the end, the hard work will pay off. Tabby and I get together, and it is as though no time has passed at all. While I have that with all of my girls, Tabby and I go back awhile longer than the rest. It gives me faith and hope that the same will occur with the rest of my girls as the years go on. Daisy is the wild card because she reminds me to be true to who I am. We both doubted at times about just being comfortable in our own skin, but she just fared much better in actually doing it than I did. She has never wavered in being who she is, no matter how wacky that may be at times. It is for that simple fact that I admire and love her so much.

I have had my fair share of scares, and it is by the grace of God that I am here. I know I have a calling in my life and He will bring it to pass (1 Thessalonians 5:24). After an infusion of confidence, I realize I deserve the best God has to offer in everything. For too long, I believed and accepted the standards that many had imposed upon me. For the longest time, I did not believe I deserved the best looking or the nicest or that I simply had to settle for one or the other. I had to be satisfied with one or the other. I have since realized that to be a lie. God knows the thoughts and plans he has for my life. They are good! He has peace and hope and a future for me (Jeremiah 29:11). That is exciting to me; I cannot wait to see how it all unfolds. I am proud of the woman I have become. I can even look in the mirror and instead of seeing what needs to be changed, I see a beautiful woman who has seen a lot in a short period of time. Thankfully, I choose not to let it defeat me. I was knocked down, but I chose to get back up. I realized it truly was and is worth fighting for. Through it all, I found the words to say, "I have fallen and been picked up. I have bent but not broken. I been lost and then found. I am still here standing, in all my natural beauty. Thank you for letting the real me come through." We all have our problems and baggage, but that is what makes us who we are.

I know my story is just one of many. I could tell of countless other people who went through the pain and hurt that I experienced in high school, at the hands of the same people who were in our lives, supposedly supporting us and helping us to grow. Unfortunately, many of those same people told them they would never make it. Those same people told them to give up and throw in the towel. Those same people gave up on them and focused on the more promising students and individuals. Those same people hurt them to the point that many no longer want anything to do with God because if that is what Christianity is all about, they can keep it. It breaks my heart to know I was not the only one, but for the grace of God, I had a family and support system around me to counter all the negativity. I was blessed to go to a Christian university where I saw firsthand how those who call themselves Christians should really act—with love. I was bathed in a love unlike any other while at Liberty, and I continue to carry that love with me. To those hurting and still carrying the wounds of yesterday, hang on. Do not give up the faith.

With all of that said and done, the question is: what is the most powerful thing I have learned so far? It can be summed up in one simple word—forgiveness. You see, I had to first learn how to forgive others. Many have hurt me, and I could have held on to that anger and bitterness and tried to use it against them, but how would that have benefitted me? The chances of people actually thinking they did anything wrong are slim at best, and holding on to that pain was just hurting me. I finally had to forgive them of all wrong and get that peace of mind for my own well-being. I knew I needed God to forgive me for holding on to the anger and bitterness for so long, but I just desperately wanted to see them hurt the way they hurt me. I now realize that I may never see any of those people getting that vengeance God promised (Romans 12:19), but I know that he will repay. Have I forgotten? No, and I doubt I will, but I refuse to let injustices of yesterday affect the promises of today and tomorrow.

Now, while forgiving other people is great, learning to forgive myself took some time. I know I wronged many people, and while they forgave me, it took a long time for me to realize that I had not forgiven myself. I, for so long, believed myself to be so horrible and maybe even unforgivable, that I carried the guilt and shame of it all even long after. I had to learn that I am not perfect—far from it (ask my family and friends), but I am also not this horrible person that many tried to get me to believe I was. I make mistakes just like everyone else, and I fall on occasion. When I fall though, I am determined to get back up and make the best of the situation. If God can forgive me, my family and friends can forgive me, then I most definitely can forgive myself.

So what does tomorrow hold for me? I have no idea. Honestly, I refuse to be overly concerned with it. I spent so much time worrying about tomorrow that I forgot to live today, and before I knew it, today became yesterday, and I looked back realizing how much time I spent worrying about nothing and getting nothing done. I know the dreams I have and goals that I want to achieve. I know that with God's help, I will be able to do just that. I have learned that if I do my part in things, He will do His. I trust He will provide even in the little things and that He will watch over and protect me. Look at all I have been through. Can I honestly say that He has not been there for me all along? I would not dare. I have seen Him in a beautiful sunrise, in the many stars on a clear night, in the smile of a newborn, in the tears while facing the death of a loved one, and in the uncertainty of an illness that had me so scared I do not know what would happen next. Through it all He has been there, and He will continue to be there. This is not the end, but rather the beginning of a new chapter. I do not believe I have a set destiny. I believe I have a set goal. Destiny is just the path I choose to take me there. I am excited to see where that path will take me. The ride alone will prove to be an interesting one. I finally realized my voice was there all along. I just had to use it.